THE QUEEN'S MAN

To my wife Cherry,
for her loving help, strength and support
at all times,
not only in the preparation of this book.

The Queen's Man

James Hepburn,
Earl of Bothwell
and Duke of Orkney
1536-1578

Humphrey Drummond

LESLIE FREWIN OF LONDON

By the same author:

OUR MAN IN SCOTLAND

First published in Great Britain in 1975
by
Leslie Frewin Publishers Limited,
Five Goodwin's Court,
Saint Martin's Lane,
London WC2N 4LL, England.

Set in Garamond
Photoset, printed and bound by
Weatherby Woolnough, Wellingborough,
Northants

ISBN 0 85632 164 8

Acknowledgements

I AM GREATLY indebted to many people for their unstinted help in the preparation of this study of one of history's bravest, most romantic and tragic heroes. It is not the first account of his life, and will not, I hope, be the last.

Over a bottle of wine from his own Hampshire vineyard, Colonel Gore-Browne took up much of his time to discuss many aspects of Bothwell with me. His own *Lord Bothwell,* published over thirty years ago, is still essential reading for anyone interested in the subject, and *The Queen's Man* is in no way intended to supersede this. It is merely a different interpretation of Bothwell's life and character.

Many of Bothwell's collateral descendants have given all the assistance they could in referring to family papers, histories and legends. The secretaries and officers of historical and topographical societies in many parts of the country have borne most patiently and helpfully with my researches. The directors and their staffs of libraries and museums, both local and national, have likewise given most learned and friendly help. Without this, there would doubtless be even more gaps in the story than appear at present. Archivists in Britain, France, Sweden, Denmark, and Germany have also been most helpful.

Among all the many people whom I would like to acknowledge individually are the Countess of Sutherland; Sir Robert Mackworth-Young, Librarian of Windsor Castle; Dr Roy Strong, Director of the Victoria and Albert Museum; Major Michael Crichton-Stuart, former Chairman of the National Trust for Scotland and Hereditary Keeper of Falkland Palace; Mr R E

Hutchison, Keeper of the Scottish National Portrait Gallery; Mr James Allan Ford, Keeper, and Mr Anderson, of the Scottish Record Office; the staff of the Department of Manuscripts in the British Museum; Mr C F Palmstierna, Private Secretary to HM the King of Sweden; Dr L Tomner, Keeper of the Archives at Malmo; Dr Johan Jorgenson, Keeper of the Archives at Copenhagen; M le Prince de Broglie, of l'Institut de France; M le Marquis de Quinsonas; Colonel Thorwald Lindquist - a full list would be a very long one.

I can only say how grateful I am to everyone who has helped me in any way with this reassessment of Bothwell's career. This naturally includes the staff of the London Library: without their unfailing courtesy and efficiency, it would of course be almost impossible to carry out any comprehensive historical research at all.

Humphrey Drummond

Megginch Castle, 1975

I

THE MORNING OF Sunday, 19th August 1561, came damply to the rough stone quay of Leith, port of Edinburgh. The mists which had folded the eastern sea-lanes in clammy cloud for the last two days dissolved into steady rain. At about nine o'clock a dainty figure stepped on to the slimy pier among the nets and old fishpots. This was Mary, lately Queen of France, and now Queen of Scots, returning to take up her inheritance.

Huddled with her, against the increasing downpour, were her magnificent uncles who had come across with her from Calais: the Duc d'Aumale, Duc François de Lorraine, and the warrior Marquis d'Elboeuf. There was no one to meet her. No preparations had been made. She was not expected then. For two hours the superbly-decked party waited to be received. Fishermen, yokels and passers by gaped at the now bedraggled splendour of renaissance France. Finally, a motley collection of horses and ponies, commandeered in the suburbs, was assembled. Mary and her party, their spirits as limp as their cambrics and brocade, clattered up the litter-laden cobbles of old Edinburgh to the palace of Holyrood. Here there was little to raise their morale or remind them of home. Rough boards, many glassless windows, a few sticks of primitive furniture. Groups of ruffians in bristling homespun jostled them in the draughty corridors.

For Mary, the vision of her triumphant homecoming dimmed rapidly. She found no echo of the courts of Versailles, Fontainebleau and Amboise, which she had been led to expect. No warm and loyal welcome from the nobles and people.

Her half-brother, Lord James Stewart, was the only one to offer

7

her any such civility. But his feelings were mixed. He saw himself on the throne: his welcome was half-hearted.

Had Mary realised what a welter of treachery, self-seeking and hypocrisy awaited her in Scotland, it is very doubtful whether she would ever have left France. The enmity and malice of her mother-in-law, Catherine de Medici, would have been a far easier cross to bear.

For of all the nobles and commoners of Scotland who revolved in fitful orbit round the throne, there was not a single true friend to whom she could turn, not one man – or woman – whom she could trust with her whole heart, except one. This was James Hepburn, Fourth Earl of Bothwell.

Like a golden straw in a gutter, his name comes floating through the murk of Scotland of the 1560s.

No one has been so consistently reviled throughout the centuries as James Bothwell. Successive writers have followed the well-worn trail of lies and misrepresentation which led to his condemnation.

But closer study suggests that he could readily take his place with the great heroes of history. For his queen, he set at risk his influence, his vast possessions, his honour and his life. For her he knew he might lose them. And for her he lost them all.

2

BOTHWELL'S GRANDFATHER, ADAM, was killed at Flodden in 1513, no more than a lad of twenty-one. But he was man enough to have sired a son by a dark-haired girl called Agnes, herself the result of a light-hearted romp by the Earl of Buchan.

This son was Bothwell's father, Patrick. Fair-whiskered and tubercular, Patrick was 'the most vain and insolent man in the world, full of folly, pride and nothing to be esteemed'. This was the opinion of Sir Ralph Sadleir, the wily agent of Henry VIII and a good judge of character. Patrick married a girl also called Agnes, daughter of Lord Sinclair and of a former Miss Hepburn. This Miss Hepburn was the outcome of a fleeting extra-marital affair between grandfather Adam Bothwell and Mary of Gueldres, widow of the Scottish King James II. Bothwell husbands and wives came together with a fine disregard for the trivialities of legal wedlock. This was the fashion of the times. Lack of marriage lines, or a too-close family relationship between couples, was discovered and denounced only when divorce was being sought.

To Patrick and Agnes a son, James, was born about 1536. Later came a daughter, called Janet. This son was James Hepburn, soon to become Fourth Earl of Bothwell, and a name to conjure with indeed. Long centuries after the kings, politicians, and intriguers of the times are no more than desiccated entries in a journal, the word 'Bothwell' never fails to arouse emotion. Throughout the most desperate struggles which man can endure Patrick's young son was to remain faithful to the cause he chose to the long and bitter end.

But it was not at his father's side that James Bothwell learnt the standards on which he patterned his life. Loyalty and integrity were qualities unknown to Patrick, Third Earl of Bothwell. A chance of winning the hand of Mary of Lorraine, Queen Dowager and widow of James V, had flashed before Patrick's pink-rimmed eyes. The existence of his devoted wife, baby son and daughter, seemed to him the only impediment. He pushed through a divorce from Agnes on the convenient score of too-close relationship. To many Scottish people, such matters were deeply shocking, and they noted with approval the complete failure of Patrick's efforts, in competition with the Earl of Lennox, to persuade the Queen Dowager to marry him. Capering and dancing at the Queen's Court with increasing frenzy, Patrick's suit can never have been considered seriously by the royal widow.

Lennox had the benefit of considerable wealth with which to buy a great wardrobe of gay clothing. His stables were full of the finest riding horses money could buy from England and France. His skill at equitation, arms, and at many musical instruments was beyond average. His voice when singing in the arras-clad chambers of the royal apartments made many a passing sentry pause to listen.

But when Patrick, Third Earl of Bothwell, raised his voice, they paused for quite different reasons. His uncertain quavering, interspersed with gutteral catches in the throat, was compared to that of 'a peacock afflicted with rheum'. His fingers were not nimble enough on string or keyboard to separate the notes. His dancing, on the occasions he was able to elbow his way into a clearing, was little more than a shambling shuffle. To complete his grotesque appearance at Court, his clothing was more suited to the parlour of a country inn. His one and only 'best suit', of ribbed velvet, hung from his drooping shoulders with no pretence at a fit.

He soon realised the futility of his efforts and left the Court. There is no evidence he ever gave another thought to his family, after establishing his wife in modest circumstances at Morham, twelve miles from Edinburgh. 'The Lady of Morham', as she came to be known, was thought of with affection and respect by the rest of the family. She died there thirty years later, having kept it a home for her children to the utmost of her ability. Throughout the first decade of those thirty years, her son and daughter spent much of their youth there. They looked on Morham as the hub of the Hepburn wheel of fortune.

But little James, rising nine years old, could not be kept and reared in a fatherless household. For a good Christian grounding and early training in the ways a young nobleman should go, James was sent to the household of his great-uncle Patrick, Bishop of Moray. The Bishop's palace was Spynie, near Elgin. This was a very dubious establishment. The Bishop himself was variously described at the time as 'vile, lecherous, dissolute, a hideous pervert——'. Other even more revealing and unsaintly terms were used.

James seems not to have suffered unduly in these robust surroundings. Whether he benefited or not can hardly be assessed. He certainly retained enough affection for the worldly Bishop to come to him for help when hounded from Scotland twenty years later. He did not receive much help, but that may not have been the Bishop's fault. Weighed down, or possibly buoyed up, by sin and surrounded by nearly twenty of his illegitimate sons – mostly bearing the same Christian names – the priestly fornicator was finally laid to rest beneath the choir stalls of Elgin Cathedral. A modest plaque on the floor of the aisle marks the spot where he lies. Over this pass in demure daily procession the chaste little choirboys of four centuries later.

Barely ten years elapsed before great events caught up with James and launched him on his turbulent career. He had learnt French. He had also gained a working knowledge of Greek and Latin, and cultivated a neat classical handwriting of distinction. Many of his grander contemporaries never mastered this latter accomplishment. They were content to scratch indecipherable scrawls on important documents, or sometimes to try a wavering cross at approximately the right place on papers of State. Others allowed their hands to be guided entirely on these occasions by the learned clerk.

This elegant hand of young Bothwell at an early age sets him apart from the uncouth gangs of 'nobles' to whom history has, with exceptions, seen fit to grant the accolade of patriotism and statesmanship.

His appearance was fiercely ugly, strongly reminiscent of a modern Border terrier. This was certainly one of the characteristics

11

which attracted women to him. Good looks can be attractive, as also can ugliness. Plainness does not commend a man to a woman: nobody accused Bothwell of being plain, nor of lacking in looks. The impression is left that his violent, ruthless spirit could be seen, bursting from his face, as though one were looking through a peephole in a grenade. His accent was an unaffected Scots. Doctor Thomas Wilson, in his contemporary *Actio,* preferred to describe it as 'his rude utterance'. It is possible that Bothwell's undoubtedly fluent vocabulary – noted later by Sir James Melville, who frequently found himself its target – drove Dr Wilson into the ranks of Bothwell's denigrators. But the Doctor was a man by no means free from fault himself: he could therefore be expected to remark with all bias upon such a personal touch as Bothwell's accent.

As befitted a young man of action, Bothwell had little time for fancy clothes, but he liked to dress up on occasion. The only contemporary portrait of him, a miniature he commissioned of himself and his first wife, Lady Jean Gordon, shows him in smart, autumn-coloured doublet of corduroy, his sandy hair *en brosse,* a neat moustache tidily trimmed. He was often noted to be wearing an old dark riding-cloak, but this will have been normal enough and gives no further clue to his usual dress.

No personal possessions of Bothwell's have yet come to light, with the exception of two books bearing his embossed arms on the leather cover. One is *The Arithmetic and Geometry of Master Stephen de la Roche,* published in French in 1538, which he probably studied at Spynie. The other is a composite volume of two works on the principles of war, by various authorities, and Valturius's *Military Discipline,* in the original French. The latter was published in Paris in 1555.

Bothwell was a Protestant. He remained so for the whole of his life, despite many great pressures, both moral and material, to turn Catholic. His acquaintanceship with the Protestant martyr, George Wishart, may have strengthened him in the religious faith to which he held so staunchly. It was Bothwell's father, Patrick, who, as local sheriff, came by night to the house of John Cockburn of Ormiston, where Wishart had sought refuge from the persecutions of the infamous Cardinal Beaton. As the result of a handsome bribe by the Cardinal, Patrick had Wishart seized in his nightshirt, promised full protection and a safe return after enquiry. From that treacherous moment, it was only a short time to the stake and slow-burning pyre of green branches in the Bishop's courtyard.

At the Cardinal's direction, Wishart was fitted out with a black linen vest on which small pockets of gunpowder were attached at the armpits and elsewhere about his person. Lolling on the cushions of his balcony, overlooking the scene, the Prince of the Church applauded each explosion of the powder bags. But three days later, the violent death predicted for him by the dying Wishart overtook him. There was no martyr's grave in the High Street of St Andrews for him as there was for his victim. Roughly salted and piled with dung, the Cardinal's fancifully desecrated corpse paid its earthly penance. Young Bothwell would have heard these stories from men who were present at all these happenings. He may have thought he owed it to his friend, George Wishart, to carry forward the Protestant faith.

Even at that age he had no time for his rapscallion father, and followed determinedly the religion of the man his father had cheated and thrown to the wolves.

3

AT DUMFRIES ON an evening in July 1556, the lungs of Patrick, Third Earl of Bothwell, finally collapsed. For the last four years, every spluttering cough had brought the day nearer. His death emancipated his daughter, Janet, from a 'hand-fast' engagement to Robert Lauder, a swarthy, loud-voiced, small land-owner from near the Bass Rock.

'Hand-fasting' was the customary engagement ritual of the times. Janet had been forced into this on 25th July by her selfish father, who wished to reward Lauder for his help during a minor pillaging expedition the day before. The exertions of the raid proved too much for the emaciated earl. Janet waited considerately until he died before renouncing the unwelcome association.

With the passing of Patrick, Third Earl of Bothwell, his son James Hepburn, student at Spynie, became Fourth Earl of Bothwell. It was a fine inheritance for a lad of twenty. James was well worthy of it.

The Hepburns had come from the hamlet of Hebburn, near Chillingham, in Northumberland, a hundred years before. Their crest of a bridled horse commemorated the day when an Earl of Dunbar, his life in peril on a runaway horse, was clawed to safety by a menial Hepburn. A patch of land at Hailes in East Lothian was the reward, releasing the family from peasant servitude south of the Border.

Soon, more grandiose abodes sheltered the Hepburns from their less fortunate neighbours, whom they now reduced to vassals. Patrick, the Hepburn of the day, became a friend of James II of Scotland. The King soon saw the advantage of having such a family under his control. Crichton Castle, a more majestic place than Hailes, was given to Patrick. Sir William Crichton, its builder, had died childless. He had been Chancellor to James I and an ineffectual guardian of his son, James II. Patrick thus completed his ambition in life, and penetrated the ragged ranks of the nobility as First Earl of Bothwell. This admirably suited the design of the Hepburns, and of Patrick in particular.

During the next two generations, the Hepburns, now Earls of Bothwell, worked hard to widen their influence. By 1550 they controlled more land and could, if they had been able to find the money to pay them, raise more armed men than anyone in Scotland.

Unfortunately for James, the Fourth Earl, his father had been rapidly dissipating these riches so laboriously accumulated, as a result of his grotesque courtship of the royal widow. But despite such squandering, James found himself, on his father's death, one of the most influential figures in Scotland.

With his earldom came the offices of Sheriff of Berwick, Haddington and Edinburgh, together with other less judicial appointments. These included the Lord High Admiralship of Scotland, the Flag Officer of the times, had there been any fleet to command. His motto was 'Keip Trest', or 'Keep Faith', It was particularly apt.

On his father's death in 1556, Bothwell applied himself with typical vigour to the formidable task of consolidating his estates. Within a month he had left for the Continent. His goal, at which he soon arrived, was the French Court at Orleans. His stay was short, but long enough to make an impression on the young wife of the Dauphin. This was Mary Stuart, absentee Queen of Scots, then fifteen years old. Although still a child, she quickly detected in the magnetic personality of this countryman of hers the latent qualities of loyalty and decision, which were to stand her mother and herself in such good stead. She wrote as much to the Bishop of Dunblane some years later, noting that Bothwell had arrived at the French Court to see her 'immediately after his father's death'.

There is no other record of what he did or said during his brief stay. But on his return to Scotland, he seems to have become fired with a great sense of purpose. He set about welding his family domains into a miniature empire. The paralysis and disintegration which had resulted from his father's weakness and dissipation was rapidly checked. Business affairs were straightened out, land sold to pay off mortages and, in some cases, to buy better land. Relations, tenants and friends were encouraged to consider themselves part of a more corporate estate than had ever been suggested before. Even his enemies, of whom jealousy and covetousness had recruited many, had to acknowledge on several recorded occasions the qualities of leadership and efficiency which the new Earl of Bothwell displayed.

He had soon elbowed his way on to the Council seats of the nation.

Mary Stuart's mother, Mary of Lorraine, had a high opinion of him. She was officially established as Regent of Scotland during her daughter's absence in France. The records show that Bothwell was with her when the Scottish Parliament met at Stirling to declare her regency. For although she had, in fact, been governing the country for the past fifteen years, on behalf of her daughter, she had never formally been proclaimed Regent. It was only now, when the country could be seen to be splitting into factions all violently opposed to each other, that the Queen Dowager took this step to reaffirm her ebbing authority. Parliament was summoned to make this important constitutional move. But on this occasion, Parliament consisted solely of the Earl of Huntly, the Earl of Argyle and the faithful Bothwell, with a handful of minor followers.

The task of maintaining the Queen Dowager's authority, and of conducting some form of coherent government, was not easy. The absence of a vigorous King and the existence of a little-known child Queen, living in France, created the circumstances in which unscrupulous men in Scotland saw opportunities for personal profit.

There was very little that could be done in the way of actual administration. There was no standing army beyond a handful of underpaid guards at Edinburgh and Stirling castles, ill-assorted and indifferently armed. There was no navy and no civil power of any description, beyond a slender band of tax-gatherers. These were accustomed to describing themselves as acting 'on behalf of the Government'. They would have been hard put on many occasions to define who or what the 'Government' was at that particular moment. The Catholic Church, with its wide network of abbeys, cathedrals, churches and colleges, run by a legion of abbots, priests and general clergy, was the only well-defined establishment.

The other organised body in Scotland at the time was that of the French regular and mercenary forces, who were virtually in service to the Queen Dowager herself. Without them, it is doubtful whether she would have been able to remain in Scotland after the death of her husband, James V. Certainly she would have had no exercisable authority at all.

The presence of all the haughty Frenchmen was much resented throughout Scotland. Not only were they splendidly equipped from the armouries of France, but their officers occupied most of the important or lucrative posts, both military and civil. Scotsmen felt, and were, subordinate. The fact that their own incompetence and lack of mutual trust had allowed this state of affairs was ignored.

Linked with jealousy of the French was an increasingly strong feeling that the Church was becoming too powerful a tool of foreigners. Too often the prelates and other members of the hierarchy were becoming involved in scandals of the most disreputable nature. Too much land was being acquired by so-called abbots and bishops, who had no pretentions to an even remotely religious life. Many of the nobles saw in this situation an opportunity to do themselves some good at the expense of the Church, while appearing to be champions of the ordinary people.

One of the illegitimate brothers of the girl Queen Mary, Lord James Stewart was the first to see the possibilities. He gathered round him various other soldiers of fortune like himself: these included such minor figures as the Earl of Pitcairn. He then began to declare publicly that all who felt matters had gone too far out of the hands of the rightful rulers of Scotland should band together with him. They would, he proclaimed, embrace the reformed religion introduced some ten years previously into England by Henry VIII: they would sweep away all vestige of foreign interference. This action would return Scotland to her former proud independence of all foreigners. Also, but Lord James was careful not to stress this, it would leave himself as obvious choice for King. He was, after all, a son of James V. The fact that his mother, Lady Margaret Douglas, was never married to James

17

V was, he maintained, of little consequence. It was unfair that he should go through life described as 'The Bastard'. The term was mitigated a little by an amendment – 'The Royal Bastard'.

Most of Scotland's leading men rallied to him. There would be more to be got out of following a semi-royal and ruthless schemer, who actually lived in Scotland and could do an enemy great mischief, than by risking one's life and career under an ailing and ineffectual Queen Dowager linked with her absent daughter. This was their reasoning. They banded together in a powerful group, which became known as the Lords of the Congregation, or simply the Lords. It is sad to reflect that none of these men, however great or limited their influence, appeared to put the interests of their country and their rightful Queen before, or on a par with, their own self-interest.

There was only one man who could be counted on to do this. The Lords knew at once where he would consider his duty to lie. This was James Hepburn, Fourth Earl of Bothwell. It was taken for granted by the Lords that Bothwell would be loyal to the Queen. But they put their case strongly to him, inviting his co-operation. Without his support, they realised their chances of success would be much reduced.

Unfortunately for the Lords, Bothwell was not a man to intrigue and turn against his Queen. He was probably the only man of position in Scotland at the time who could not be swayed by bribery from the path of duty. This rare, perhaps unique integrity made many bitter enemies for him. Soon, all the rest of the Lords readily succumbed to the temptation of small parcels of money wrapped up in grand promises, which began to flow towards them from England.

As Bothwell was not a Catholic, he could have been expected to sympathise with the reforming aims of the Lords' programme. But he detected at once the self-advancement which was the true purpose of the Lords' campaign. The trickle of golden coins from England held them in closer thrall than Bothwell's intangible, less profitable, bonds of patriotism and loyalty.

He became their implacable enemy.

The early months of 1558 were important for Bothwell. They marked the beginning of his military career. For the Percy family, headed by the Earl of Northumberland and his brother, portly Sir

Henry, staged a raid across the Border from England. It was designed to destroy farm produce stored for the winter, and lay waste buildings and hamlets. This adventure, apart from being good sport and a traditional activity, would serve to remind the Scots that England was now allied to Spain through the marriage of Philip of Spain to Queen Mary Tudor. If Scotland wished to continue her dalliance with France, which was at war with Spain, then Scotland must take the consequences. These consequences were the bustling Percys clattering along the Border lanes, tossing firebrands into stackyards, herding sheep and cattle southwards, and, it was hoped, striking good Anglo-Spanish fear into the hearts of the Franco-Scots.

These fine plans went far astray. No one had reckoned with the Earl of Bothwell. By brilliant deployment and lightning action, the small force under his command routed the Percy brigade, although the Englishmen all but captured the Earl of Huntly in the town of Langton on which the raid was centred. Huntly had been appointed Scottish Lieutenant of the Borders by the Queen Dowager. She was disgusted at his poor showing in the early stages of the raid.

But the miniature invasion soon collapsed under the force of Bothwell's attack. It was an ignominious conclusion. The name of Bothwell was now spoken with increasing awe on both sides of the Border.

There were many people who had observed the dash and skill of the young Earl. Among them were the citizens of Edinburgh. They had been unnerved by the violence of the English forces. It would not have taken Northumberland's troops much longer to reach Edinburgh itself. The city at that time was almost defence-less. The great wall, hurriedly built at the time of Flodden, over forty years earlier, offered no protection now; it was full of holes where it had either tumbled down or where the stones had been carried off for house-building. Who was to organise a defence if attack should come? Who better than Lord Bothwell?

The citizens petitioned the Queen Dowager at once for him to be appointed captain of the city's defences, with full powers to build walls and forts and to raise troops. This was one occasion where Mary of Lorraine could achieve something. She made Bothwell Keeper of the great castle called the Hermitage, deep in the wildest and most uncontrollable sector of the Borders. This huge fortress stands today much as it did then, as grey and lonely as the mists which sweep endlessly across those wide moors. It could hold fifteen hundred men and was practically impregnable. Bothwell at once took charge. The salary of some three hundred pounds a year which went with it would not have gone far. But on his first official appointment at the hand of the Queen Dowager, and in the name of the Queen of Scots, it is not surprising that he was willing enough to provide all the extra money needed from his own resources.

But the widespread praise which Bothwell was now receiving on all sides for his military efforts aroused the professional jealousy of Seigneur d'Oysel, the Queen Dowager's French general. He persuaded her to allow him to mount a grand assault of his own against the English. The castle of Wark, just south of the river Tweed, was to be the first objective. Heavy siege guns rumbled down the rough road from Edinburgh and were set up in text-book positions. Piles of cannon balls were stacked ready; powder and supplies of all sorts were collected. The French threw them-selves delightedly into the massive preparations. The Queen Dowager herself was swept up in their enthusiasm: she took up advance headquarters at Home Castle, on a knoll which gives a wide view of what was to be the scene of operations.

But not everyone shared this enthusiasm. The Lords, uneasy at the ascendency of their new enemy, the Earl of Bothwell, and jealous of the trust and authority placed in him by the Queen Dowager, complained bitterly against the warlike preparations in general, and against the French in particular. They had another reason for trying to disrupt the impending assault. Many of them were now receiving regular bribes from England. If they appeared to co-operate in any attack upon English strongholds, they knew well enough that their squalid pension would dry up at once. The realisation of this drove them to frenzied complaints against d'Oysel and the Queen Dowager. D'Oysel knew he could make nothing of his great plans without infantry and support troops. If the Lords would not provide these, any siege work was a waste of time. There were not enough French soldiers to fill the gap. Reluctantly, d'Oysel had to recommend that the whole exercise be abandoned. He was furious, and the Queen Dowager greatly disappointed. But she made up for it to a certain extent by appointing Bothwell Lieutenant of the Borders in place of the corpulent and useless Earl of Huntly. The announcement appeared in the accounts of the Lord High Treasurer for 29th October 1558. It established Bothwell as one of the most influential and powerful men in the realm. The Lords seethed with rancour, not unmingled with apprehension. The Queen Dowager, whom they were working so hard to betray and destroy, had acquired a powerful ally.

The new Lieutenant determined to demonstrate his military skill at once. He planned an important raid himself upon the English. In order to consolidate his new command among the now sulking Frenchmen, it was to be a combined operation. He would take some eighteen hundred troops to create a diversion, while d'Oysel and his siege trains would batter the castle of Norham into submission. This was some seven miles up river from Berwick, on the south bank of the Tweed. To a certain extent the adventure was a success. By great cunning and very rapid movement, Bothwell drew out Northumberland's forces.

A day or two after Christmas was perhaps an unsporting time to choose. But it is likely that Christmas celebrations meant more to the English than to the Scots of the time. Four centuries were to elapse before Christmas could be described as a time of festivity north of the Border.

Sir Henry Percy galloped further from his base at Wooler than was wise. Bothwell was ready for him. In a steep dingle near Haltwellsweir, just south of the present village of Ford, the English party was ambushed. From contemporary descriptions, there was more shouting, bolting of horses, and wild discharging of firearms than serious business. Bothwell and his Border warriors careered after the routed Northumbrians. Soon they noticed the Earl of Northumberland himself riding importantly northwards to join his brother's scattered forces. Not wishing to have a pitched battle for no particular reason, Bothwell reined in his troops and prudently withdrew. Nothing had been achieved on the ground, but an important effect had been created of the military potential of the Scotsmen under their new Border Lieutenant.

There was one mystery about the whole affair. What had happened to the Frenchmen with their ponderous siege weapons and heavy armour? Contemporary records are silent. D'Oysel's own dispatches make no mention of the manœuvre. There is a hint of disagreement between the Queen Dowager and her French captains at this stage. Since she had returned to Edinburgh after the previous fiasco, it seems likely that d'Oysel indulged in one of his bouts of shouting and stamping his feet, causing the rest of his commanders in the field to return home smarting from insults. This had happened occasionally before. Frenchmen are notoriously quick, when in high positions, to detect supposed insults. It is certain that the French command at that time was a difficult one to maintain under such irascible leadership.

The scale of such activity from the Scottish side was taken very seriously in London. Big reinforcements were planned for the Border. The Percy family were instructed to make their defences more effective. Spies and agents were sent north to see whether the quisling Lords of Scotland could be made more efficient traitors. It had soon been recognised in London that a man of Bothwell's calibre was liable to throw out of balance the quiet ascendancy which English policy was establishing in Scotland.

But suddenly, by the death of one person, the whole political complexion was altered. Mary of England died. By her marriage to Philip of Spain, she had allied England with Spain against France, and thus against Scotland too. With Mary dead, it was no longer necessary to consider what policies Spain wished to pursue. Philip had never been considered as a worthy Consort or King in London. It is certain he was a less than successful or loving husband. With relief on the English side, negotiations for a truce, and perhaps for permanent peace, were started on the Border.

Bothwell was ready to discuss arrangements with the Earl of Northumberland. But with all likelihood of any action now being at an end, Bothwell's interest in the matter evaporated. He did meet Northumberland at least twice in the early part of 1559, but seems not to have taken the parleying at all seriously. Nothing transpired. At least, from Bothwell's point of view, nothing transpired. But had he taken a little more interest in the current fashion of intriguing with the enemy, he would have noticed a very significant development. This concerned the Laird of Grange, a good soldier on the side of the Lords, but noncommittal towards the Queen Dowager. He was to prove himself a supreme traitor before the end of the next decade. But at the moment, he was content to carry information to the Earl of Northumberland on the best way of getting more action and co-operation out of the Lords to the benefit of the English cause. His advice was sound and successful. More money. Heavy leather purses were handed over. Arrangements for peace on the Border were considered to be complete for the time being.

Oblivious or careless of such artful work behind the scenes, the Lieutenant of the Border had hung up his sword for a spell. He had made the closer acquaintance of one of the most interesting and undoubtedly fascinating women in Scotland. This was Lady Janet Scott, widow of Sir Walter Scott of Buccleuch.

It has been customary to detect something obscene in Bothwell's friendship with this lady. She was nineteen years older than Bothwell, a niece of the ruthless Cardinal Beaton, which was no fault of hers. She was a friend of the Queen Dowager and well known at Court. Had she been the lewd gorgon historians would have us believe, the Queen Dowager would have been the last to tolerate her presence. She had been married four times and borne seven children. Two of her earlier marriages had been unfortunate, but there is precedent for worthy people making unfortunate marriages. Her last husband, a man accustomed to saying what he thought of people, expressed his opinion of his neighbours, the Kerrs of Cessford, Ferniehurst and Littledean. They had not been friends for many years. One evening in 1552, Sir Walter met a party of Kerrs in the High Street in Edinburgh. The Kerrs disposed of him quietly and unkindly, also unfairly, since they were far the more numerous.

Lady Janet took quick revenge, for which she was later to gain the reputation for unpredictable violence. She collected a large body of Scott supporters and assailed a church in which an ally of the Kerrs was cowering in sanctuary. Thinking the avenging of her late husband more important than the sanctity of the church, she smashed the door herself with an axe and flung the unfortunate man of the Kerrs to the mob of her supporters.

This was not ladylike behaviour, but it did not deserve wholehearted condemnation. Women have behaved more wickedly before and since without being branded as wholly evil.

Lady Janet has been condemned for dabbling in the occult, for conjuring up strange powers, for gaining weird ascendancies over people. But it seems that she was no more than a woman with a lively, questing mind, perhaps a little ahead of her time, a forceful personality of considerable charm, and a most entertaining hostess. What could be more natural than her neighbour, the young Earl of Bothwell, striking up a close friendship with her? He was himself an outstanding and unconventional character, a man of action and lively wit. His name was on every tongue. He was a close friend of the Queen Dowager and often to be found at Court. He was the greatest landowner in the Borders and newly appointed to a position of the highest importance in that region.

Lady Janet has gained notoriety as the nonsensically named Wizard Lady of Branxholm in the writings of another, and later, Walter Scott. Branxholm Tower, much altered, stands to this day among trees and flowering shrubs above the busy road to Jedburgh.

However much of a 'wizard' she may have been, her true friendship for the young Earl of Bothwell survived that of many others, who abandoned him without adequate cause. When his great castle of Hermitage was ransacked by ruffians in the pay of the Lords in the years to come, it was Lady Janet Scott of Branxholm who provisioned the castle again at her own expense. Many times she is found giving him urgently needed help without any recompense to herself. Her example was one which others could well have followed.

It has been suggested that Bothwell went so far as to marry Lady Janet. It certainly seems they were 'hand-fast' engaged. It was only necessary to clasp hands before witnesses and to declare oneself engaged. After a trial period this could lead naturally to marriage, or the relationship was dissolved, again before witnesses.

In April 1559, it is recorded that Bothwell was sitting in judgement on the local court in his capacity as sheriff of the district. A man brought a case against Lady Janet before this court. On finding Bothwell the judge, the man bringing the case complained that the judge could not be impartial, since he had been 'quietly married or hand-fast' to Lady Janet. This must either have been true, or at least widely believed, since Bothwell is recorded as having stepped down for a deputy to try the case.

The fact remains that Bothwell's friendship with her was an

enduring one, with none of the squalid overtones with which so many writers have tried to befoul it.

Later in the summer of the same year, 1559, more negotiations were attempted to establish conditions of permanent peace along the Borders. Bothwell was again in charge of the Scottish party. His old adversary, Sir Henry Percy, spoke for the English, accompanied by Cuthbert Tunstall, Bishop of Durham. But like so many meetings between the representatives of nations, the most trivial matter occupied their whole attention. No agenda was ever discussed, since neither side could agree on the exact spot where the meeting should take place. Bothwell insisted on Scottish soil. Sir Henry insisted on English soil. To break the deadlock, the Bishop of Durham suggested the flat tables of rock which lie in midstream, so characteristic of certain reaches of the river Tweed. The laughable charade took up so much time, and nearly drowned the Bishop in his heavy robes as he slipped more than once into the reedy current among the trout and June salmon, that the parley was abandoned. It seems that Bothwell's sense of humour was possibly to blame, since the record shows a complaint to the Queen Dowager about the conduct of affairs. Sir Henry asked urgently for a 'wise and discreet' gentleman to be sent to represent the Scottish side.

The Queen probably enjoyed the joke with Bothwell, since she declined to make any alteration in her representatives.

But before matters had time to deteriorate any further, an event of importance occurred in France. King Henry of France crashed dead to the ground at a tournament, killed accidentally by a splintered lance. His young son Francis came uncertainly to the throne, pale, weak, and constantly suffering from headaches. The only real comfort and joy in his life was his even younger wife. This was Mary Stuart, Queen of Scots, and now Queen of France as well. For the coronation, the Queen Dowager in Edinburgh appointed Bothwell as her representative. She was now relying very heavily on him for exercising what authority she could still command in Scotland. They both knew well enough what the Lords were planning to do. The Lords were nearly a party in open rebellion and could not be trusted in any way. Spies had revealed to the Queen Dowager many of their plans: she was well aware of the bribes and pensions being received by the traitors. She realised also that the recent prevarications by the English over the Border negotiations were simply because they were hoping to find, and recommend to her as acceptable, delegates among the Lords who could be relied on to betray her to them.

When the wily Sir Ralph Sadleir took charge of the English side, her suspicions were confirmed. She went to the length of complaining openly to Sir Henry Percy at the way his side was treating with, and encouraging, her 'rebels'.

But despite these difficulties, a treaty was drawn up and agreed. Bothwell signed for Scotland, Sir Ralph Sadleir, Sir Henry Percy, and the discomfited Bishop of Durham for England.

Little attention was paid to its provisions. But it was better than having no treaty at all. It showed what could be done if anyone concerned would agree to keep the peace.

4

IN ENGLAND A formidable political partnership was being established. This was the new Queen, Elizabeth, and her principal Secretary of State, Sir William Cecil. Between them they ran the country. The detailed network of spies and informers, which Cecil established all over the country, is well known and fully documented. The mountain of papers and letters which survive to this day, many carefully annotated by Cecil himself, proves the efficiency of what amounted to a Secret Service unparalleled in the sixteenth century.

It was through these sources that the state of affairs in Scotland was clearly interpreted in London. Queen Elizabeth had probably made up her mind early in life not to marry. Her experiences, before she came to the throne, at the hands of Thomas Seymour had given her little encouragement in this respect. It is also possible that she knew herself to be incapable of childbirth. But whatever the truth of these intimate details, Elizabeth never had far from her thoughts the problem of who should succeed her on the throne of England. Mary Stuart was the legitimate heir, being the great-niece of Elizabeth's father, Henry VIII, and Elizabeth's next nearest relation. Mary was, of course, a staunch Catholic, whereas Elizabeth had continued in the reformed Protestant faith established by her father. Whom Mary would marry was an important question for Elizabeth. The English Queen was also concerned with the succession to the Scottish throne. It was not at all convenient to have such a powerful French presence across the border personified by the Queen Dowager, Mary of Lorraine. Cecil frequently pointed out to his Queen that a reliable Protestant on the Scottish throne, with no attachment to France in any way, would be preferable to the young Mary Queen of Scots in due course, and to her mother, the Queen Dowager, at present.

For this reason Elizabeth was readily persuaded to start the system of bribing the Scottish Lords in order to induce the expulsion of the Queen Dowager, and the collapse of French influence in Scotland. Such a state of affairs would also preclude the return to Scotland of Mary Stuart. Cecil had no difficulty in explaining the validity of a claim to the Scottish throne by the head of the Hamilton family, the Duke of Châtelherault. Or, if he was rather beyond it, then of his son, James, Earl of Arran.

Arran was in the early stages of the madness which eventually caused him to be locked up for the rest of his life. But this need not trouble Elizabeth, as Cecil explained to her. It might even make him easier to deal with, since he would have no opinions of his own to conflict with those of his English neighbours.

As usual, Cecil knew how best to work for the dissolution of Scottish authority. More bribes were needed. Elizabeth was notoriously reluctant to sanction the payment of anything at all, even of properly presented State or Household accounts. Many of her servants and officials went for long periods without their salaries or expenses. The costs of the army and navy frequently had to be borne for an embarrassing time by the generals and admirals concerned. To persuade her to produce large sums of money for subtle and secret bribes in Scotland fully taxed Cecil's ingenuity. But he achieved his object in the end, although not so fully as he had hoped.

He explained that substantial sums paid now to the restive and treacherous Lords might well swing the whole balance in Scotland in favour of Elizabeth's nominee. Had she agreed to the massive sums suggested, there is little doubt that the plans for subversion would have come near success. But she would agree this time only to an instalment of 3,157 French crowns. It was to be in French money to disguise its origin.

A strong hint was sent by Cecil to Scotland that a heavy infusion of English gold could shortly be expected. But before the money was to be delivered, he indicated that Her Majesty would be glad to see some positive action taken by her associates to set the programme of disruption in motion.

Sir Ralph Sadleir, the envoy who knew Scotland and the Scots better than many Scotsmen themselves, conveyed this message to Lord James Stewart. Lord James had unchallenged control of his Lords. He considered himself a suitable candidate for Regent of Scotland once the Queen Dowager could be removed with all her Frenchmen. He then proposed to rule in the absence of Mary Stuart, Queen of Scots. He was certain in his own mind that he could either ensure the permanent absence of the young Queen, his half-sister, or if she did return, reduce her to complete dependence upon him.

Elizabeth's promise of money was all that was needed to start the whole operation. In October 1559, the Lords finally came out in open rebellion against the Queen Dowager. They gathered in Edinburgh, of which they took occupation, declared themselves the true ruling party of Scotland, and issued a proclamation divesting the Queen Dowager of all authority to govern.

The few remaining Scotsmen loyal to the Queen Dowager, together with all the available French troops, withdrew to the old fortified town of Leith, the port of Edinburgh, in which they prepared to resist a siege. The Queen Dowager herself, increasingly ill with dropsy, remained in Edinburgh Castle. The courage of the rebel Lords did not extend to laying hands upon her.

Cecil was delighted. The three thousand French crowns were packed into a leather bag and dispatched north to reward the loyal servants of Elizabeth for their first manœuvre. It reached Berwick safely. Here it was put in the capable hands of a man called John Cockburn, of Ormiston. An ardent supporter of the Lords, Cockburn was especially suited for the important task of delivering the money into the eager hands of the waiting Lords. For Cockburn had recently signed a solemn document pledging his devoted service to the Queen Dowager. It was this Cockburn's house where the martyr George Wishart had taken refuge some years before. It was he who had betrayed Wishart's whereabouts to Patrick Hepburn, the Fair Earl, father of James, the present and Fourth Earl of Bothwell. In addition, the Queen Dowager had just restored to Cockburn his lands, which he had forfeited not long before for giving aid to the English during a Border dispute.

Cockburn tucked into his belt the two hundred crowns which

he received from Sir Ralph Sadleir for his work of courier. Across his saddle bow he slung the bulky leather bag. It was a dark and wintry October night. Cockburn and the seven men of his bodyguard trotted confidently through the gloom. Half the journey done, they came down the fold of the valley towards the town of Haddington.

Without any warning, a few silent horsemen were among them in a second. Cockburn's men scattered. A stocky figure knocked him flying with the flat of a blade. Another swift cut across his saddle and the precious portmanteau was wrenched free. Within moments of appearing like a wraith, Her Majesty's Lieutenant of the Border had as rapidly vanished into the night towards Crichton Castle. Across his own saddle lay the bag of secret English gold.

For Cockburn's mission had not been a secret as he, or Sir Ralph Sadleir, or the Lords had imagined. Word had soon come to Bothwell that another instalment of 'traitors' pay' was coming north to cheer the rebels. He at once informed the Queen Regent. She approved his plan to snatch the money and devote it to the maintenance of her own treasury. This forced gift from Elizabeth of England would have given her cause for wry amusement. For Bothwell, it was one more opportunity to serve his Queen and strike a vigorous blow at the plans of the rebel Lords, whom he had now come so much to despise. It was also fun to carry out. There is evidence throughout Bothwell's life that he got as much fun out of it as he could.

He soon reached the initial safety of Crichton Castle. Doubtless the story of the raid was well received and lost little in the telling. Curiously, Bothwell must have stayed in his castle without posting distant guards, and believing that no one would know who had carried out the raid. But he had been recognised even in that short space of time. Word was carried very quickly to the rebels in Edinburgh of the loss of their gold. The identity of the highwayman was established equally soon. With unaccustomed vigour, Lord James Stewart and the shambling Earl of Arran dashed out of Edinburgh with nearly two hundred men behind them.

Bothwell was not prepared for such an immediate reaction. He was still in his slippers and no horse saddled when the rebel force was announced barely fifteen minutes away. Without stopping to put on his boots or have his horse saddled, Bothwell raced into the courtyard, vaulted on to the barebacked charger and galloped eastwards over the low grassy hills, back towards Haddington. Firmly clamped on the horse's withers was the leather bag of gold. The rebels came surging round the castle, but their man was gone. Arran and Lord James Stewart spent the night in Crichton. No attempt had been made, very wisely, to keep them out. A party was sent after Bothwell, but he gave then the slip in the narrow lanes and back regions of the little town of Haddington.

Finally, like a hunted hare, he doubled back on his tracks, ran down the course of the little stream at the back of the town and darted through the waterside doorway of a house. The Hepburn family preserve the legend that the astonished householder was by chance a friend called Sandybed. Bothwell quickly changed clothes with a girl working in the kitchen and carried on with the work she had been doing. He thus escaped detection, remaining in the house for some days until it was safe to emerge. It is recorded that Bothwell expressed his gratitude by ordering four bags of grain to be paid annually to the family of Sandybed. A record which seems reliable enough shows that this payment was made from the Hepburn family estates until the middle of the eighteenth century.

Bothwell had escaped with his life and the money, but he was not unscathed. Lord James and Arran had themselves withdrawn from Crichton Castle, but had left a garrison of fifty men. They declared that unless Bothwell made amends to his unfortunate cousin, James Cockburn, and gave up the bag of money to them, Crichton Castle would be sacked and all Bothwell's belongings carried off. Needless to say, Bothwell ignored them and held on to the money until he could hand it over to the Queen Dowager.

The departure of Lord James from Edinburgh with his two hundred men had been observed from the now beleaguered town of Leith. The French general, d'Oysel, took the opportunity of making an unexpected and violent sally from the town. He captured two siege guns which had been spasmodically pounding the walls, and did a great deal of damage to the rebel forces which had been conducting the siege. He even drove the remainder of their force the four miles back to Edinburgh itself, before withdrawing in triumph behind the walls of Leith.

By way of retaliation, Lord James sent more troops to Crichton and carried out his threat to destroy it. He first took away all the movables. It is particularly recorded that the chief item was Bothwell's charter chest. In this would have been most of the deeds of his extensive properties. The Castle was then set on fire. Powerless at the moment to intervene, Bothwell watched from the roof of Borthwick Castle, a stout and lofty tower no more than two or three miles away. This belonged to his friend and neighbour. The castle still belongs to the Borthwicks, and remains almost completely unchanged from that time. Unlike so many houses and castles, now, alas, including Crichton itself, Borthwick is still lived in.

The ignominious loss of their dishonourable money, the universal disclosure of its source, and the serious reverse they had suffered in front of the town of Leith, all served to demoralise the rebel force. Many of them were doubtless feeling a sense of guilt at their treacherous behaviour. This guilt could only satisfactorily be overcome by handsome payments: if the money was not even to be forthcoming, and they were to be routed in the field, then perhaps the whole adventure was a mistake. Doubts were cast on the efficiency of Lord James and his worth as a leader. Arran was already becoming an object of derision in the uncertain state of his mind.

In addition to all this, the Frenchmen surged out yet again from Leith, scattering the besiegers like blood-stained chaff. The rank and file of the rebels began to slink away. The leaders lost their nerve. At midnight after the second sortie from Leith, the remainder of the rebels gathered up what forces they had left and stole away to Stirling.

The Queen Dowager was back in command, at least for the time being. The man who had cracked the morale of her enemies was the Earl of Bothwell. She never forgot the efforts he made on her behalf. Witnesses who recorded her manner when Bothwell was with her noted her great tenderness towards him. She was a woman capable of deep gratitude: this she would have shown fully to her gallant Lieutenant of the Border.

32

5

FOR BOTHWELL AND the cause of the Queen Dowager, the events of the previous few weeks had been encouraging. The rebels appeared to be in disarray. But Cecil was not one to accept such reverses without profiting by them. He realised at once that the instalments of money were not going to achieve results. One could not even guarantee their safe delivery while the Earl of Bothwell was on the prowl. The rebel Lords appeared to lack the fibre necessary to act on their own. The time had come, Cecil decided, for more massive and direct action, in the name of the Queen of England, to rid Scotland of the French and to place the Earl of Arran on the throne. He therefore made preparations for the invasion of Scotland by land and sea.

In Scotland, Bothwell knew well enough that Cecil would not allow the rebels to disintegrate. Reports soon reached the Queen Dowager that a combined force was being raised in England for a sinister purpose.

As was always the case with Bothwell, his first inclination was to take direct action himself. He could never have been described as a subtle schemer. He cared little for diplomatic manœuvres: in his opinion, a sharp sword, a light suit of armour and a nimble horse would settle all questions of policy or statesmanship. He accordingly issued a challenge to the Earl of Arran, accusing him of disloyalty to the Crown and treason to the State. With Arran honourably slain, the field would be clearer for the next operation. The chief opponent of the Queen Dowager and her daughter would be eliminated, and the English plot greatly weakened. From a more personal point of view, it would be satisfactory to be able to avenge the sacking of Crichton Castle.

Arran was appalled at this threat of personal involvement with Bothwell. Speechless with alarm on receipt of the challenge, he collapsed, grey with sweat and trembling from head to foot. His father extricated him from this unnerving situation by replying to Bothwell, in Arran's name, that he would not demean himself to take up the challenge, and did not anyway consider that he had anything to answer for. In quavering defiance – for his father also had no wish to receive a similar challenge which he might find difficult in avoiding – Arran suggested that Bothwell had forfeited the right to meet honourably in combat by his midnight escapade. Only when adequate amends had been made would Arran be prepared to reconsider the challenge.

Bothwell shrugged the matter off. He turned his attention to Cockburn, the courier whom he had relieved of the money. The Queen Dowager could not afford to lose what few supporters she had. It was urgent to build up more throughout the country if she was to maintain her regained authority. There were barely three thousand Frenchmen and little more than a thousand or two of Scotsmen. The more who could be won over to her the better.

Bothwell went to see Cockburn, now practically recovered from the rough treatment he had received at the hands of his cousin. It was Bothwell's aim to win the firm support of all his friends and relations, and gradually to build a solid foundation for a régime which could not be overthrown by the rebels. He hoped that, if only this could be established, the rebels would give up their alliance with England and devote themselves wholeheartedly to their own country.

Cockburn received him politely enough. He could not have expected open arms, but at least they made peace between them. With other members of the family and various kinsmen and their friends, Bothwell made some progress in the winning of vital support.

While this was going on, spies were almost daily bringing reports to the Queen Dowager of Cecil's and Elizabeth's preparations for invasion. It was now beyond conjecture. The situation was extremely serious for the Queen Dowager and her chief supporter, Bothwell. If they were not to be swept away by an English horde and the country handed over to the rebel Lords, something drastic would have to be done.

The first step was to safeguard the vital supply lines from France, and greatly increase the volume of aid at once. This could be done only by ensuring that the eastern approaches were in loyal hands. To do this, Bothwell proposed to garrison the towns along the Firth of Forth leading from the open sea direct to Edinburgh and Leith. With these secured, and the French ready to give almost unlimited help, it might be possible to stem, even to turn back, the English when they came in the spring.

The second step was to neutralise the remaining rebel forces as soon as possible, before they had time to regain their lost morale, or to receive substantial reinforcements from England.

To achieve these two objects at one stroke, Bothwell and the Queen Dowager decided on a bold military sweep of the eastern kingdom of Fife, which included the most important seaboard, and a lesser expedition along the southern shore of the Firth of Forth.

The elaborate preparations for this expedition included plans for the sacking of the Hamilton family headquarters of Kinniel Castle, in return for the loss of Crichton, which Bothwell had felt deeply. The Earl of Arran and his father might both, with any luck, be found at home. Lord James Stewart might also be caught somewhere along the route.

D'Oysel was delighted at the prospect of getting his Frenchmen into action on his own terms. The small army was soon ready. The sweep eastwards from Edinburgh was put under way, with Stirling included in the plans for occupation.

Most curiously, nothing is heard of Bothwell once the force got on the move. No record has yet come to light to explain why Bothwell took no further part for at least a month. His name does not appear on any list, either civil or military. No one seems to have wondered where he was or commented on his absence. To add to the mystery, a reference is found to him in a report to Cecil from the notorious spy, Thomas Randolph. In the second week of December 1559, his regular dispatch contains the question: 'What shall be done, said or written to the Earl of Bothwell?' Cecil replied in his spidery writing: 'If he cannot be won from the French, practice the taking of him.'

This is a clear instruction to kidnap or otherwise capture Bothwell. Randolph would have known the futility of trying to bribe him to desert his Queen. Likewise there would have been no opportunity to abduct him by force or guile as long as he was in command of troops in the field. It is evident, therefore, that Bothwell cannot at this stage have been taking part in the warlike operations through Fife. He would never have allowed the excesses of violence and cruelty to which the French troops gave full rein throughout the whole of the minor campaign.

He must either have been ill, in which case it would hopefully have been reported at once to Cecil. There are no such reports in the unbroken chronology of Cecil's papers. Or he may have gone abroad, but this would be very unlikely at this critical stage in the Queen Dowager's affairs. He is known to have gone abroad a little later, and is unlikely to have gone away twice in that space of time. He might have had a disagreement with the French over plans for the Fife campaign and retired to the Borders for it to take its course without him. This is possible, since there were always matters on the Borders which needed his attention, either to do with his own properties or connected with raising support for the Queen Dowager. Perhaps judicial work, arising from his Lieutenancy of the Border, required his presence there. Had this been the case, it is likely that his attendance at some court or conference at Kelso, Jedburgh, or other centre would have been recorded at the time. A scrutiny of all available Border documents has failed to reveal a mention of his name during this period.

Could he have taken French leave and become involved in some affair of the heart, obliging him to retire briefly from official work? This seems far fetched. Although perfectly capable of an adventure of this nature, he would hardly have been able to remain hidden without comment or discovery for so long at a time like this. Randolph again noted Bothwell's absence in his next dispatch to Cecil. The spy also informed his master that Bothwell's sister, Janet, and become involved in some scandal. Unfortunately, he was reluctant to record the details, 'because,' he wrote, 'you will judge it to be but a merry matter. I will leave it to a further time, though it is worth the reporting.' It has not been possible to throw any light on this incident. Bothwell himself may have been involved in the scandal, whatever it was, and may have spent the missing weeks in that way. But if this had been the case, one would have expected Randolph to link his name more closely with it. In his dispatches, which seem to survive in unbroken sequence, Randolph does not take the story any further and makes no more mention of Bothwell at that stage.

It has been impossible to produce an explanation of his disappearance, for so long at such an important time, which has any evidence to support it. The most reasonable conjecture, based on no more than guess-work, is that he fell out with the French over their savage campaign in Fife, and withdrew in ill humour to the Borders until he had to return to the ailing Queen Dowager. This is not very much in character. It can only be hoped that some direct evidence will one day be found to solve the mystery.

In Bothwell's absence, the French troops blazed through the countryside, killing and pillaging. The remaining forces of the Lords fell back before them, unable to do anything to stem the advance. Lord James and Arran found themselves left with barely two hundred men. Lord James must have felt greatly discouraged, burdened with the increasing madness of his joint commander, and having the majority of his troops desert him. He knew well enough of the scale of the impending invasion by his English allies. If only he could hold on until they arrived, the tide would very soon be turned. It was doubtless this knowledge alone that made him struggle on.

Meanwhile the French swept on towards the final port of St Andrews. Its capture would consolidate the twin coast lines along the supply route, and ensure the steady and uninterrupted flow of men and materials of war promised from France.

But when the French were only a few miles short of St Andrews, the whole situation changed suddenly and dramatically. A large fleet of armaments and troops sent from France came to complete disaster off the Dutch coast. The ships were dispersed or wrecked and many hundreds of soldiers were drowned. Only one vessel struggled into Leith with a hundred exhausted men on board. These were the reinforcements upon which the Queen Dowager's men were relying for the final elimination of the rebel Lords and for meeting the English invasion. Some twenty small vessels had from time to time landed supplies from France for them, but the now wrecked fleet had carried the main hope. When fourteen men-of-war at last sailed into the Firth one January morning of that year, 1560, the Frenchmen were delighted. These were surely the forerunners of the massive reinforcements promised by the King of France. The Frenchmen, ready to overwhelm St Andrews and consolidate the coast, would see to it that Scotland was held for Catholicism. The realm now under the protection of Mary of Lorraine, Queen Dowager and Regent on behalf of Mary, Queen of Scotland and of France, would be in safe hands, preserved from the clutches of the jealous Elizabeth of England.

But the delight of the Frenchmen turned quickly to dismay as the standard of St George of England was seen to break from the flagship. The leading vessels opened fire on the supply ships lying at Leith, sinking or capturing all of them. It was the English flotilla under Admiral Winter, forerunners of the threatened English invasion.

Alarm developed into chaos and dismay. From conquerors sweeping all before them, the Frenchmen had become an isolated army with cut supply lines. D'Oysel realised at once that his adventure was over, that unless he got back quickly to Leith the local population, stiffened by the few rebel troops, would destroy him and his men. With his supplies so suddenly denied him, he could not possibly hold out. He therefore gave up the campaign at once and dashed back to Leith as fast as he could get his troops to move. There was no alternative but to reoccupy the now battered old town of Leith and prepare to resist the land forces of the English, which were rumoured to be on the way. There was now no more hope of receiving supplies from the sea.

The one encouraging event was the reappearance of the Earl of Bothwell, as sudden as had been his disappearance. Morale was apt to recover very rapidly in his company: the Frenchmen set to work repairing the meagre defences and getting ready for yet another siege.

The Queen Dowager remained in Edinburgh Castle, now scarcely able to leave her bed because of the dropsy. But despite her illness, she conferred daily with Bothwell. Between them, they did what they could to rally the country in the face of such a serious threat from across the Border. She called on all men of loyalty and goodwill to come forward in defence of their Queen and country. Those who gave aid to the English were proclaimed traitors, and Arran was arraigned for being the ringleader of an illegal rebellion.

Before long a herald arrived from Elizabeth with a formal declaration of war. On 30th March, the large army which had been quartered at Newcastle and Berwick crossed the Scottish border. Like jackals in the wake of a hunting lion, Lord James Stewart and Arran brought their furtive ragged troops out of the shadows to join the English commander, Lord Grey de Wilton. The Duke of Norfolk was theoretically the Commander-in-Chief, but few people had detected evidence of military skill or martial knowledge in his career so far. Elizabeth and Cecil had given him the honourable appointment in order to secure his wavering loyalty to Elizabeth. The Duke had taken the precaution of signing a bond of alliance with Lord James and Arran, by which he hoped to ensure their loyalty to the English cause during the forthcoming campaign. He evidently had as little experience of Lord James Stewart as he had of military affairs. He would otherwise not have wasted the parchment and ink.

The large force moved unopposed to the gates of Leith. There was, of course, no one to oppose them in the name of the Queen Dowager. Every man of loyalty was behind the tumbledown walls, building them up as fast as he could. From the lofty rampart of Edinburgh Castle, the valiant Queen Dowager gazed down on the scene four miles away. Each day she was wheeled out on a litter until her doctor forbade her to be moved.

Pulsing inside the old town, like a time-bomb with a shortening fuse, Bothwell fumed at his lack of an adequate army with which to drive the invaders from his beloved Scotland. Twice he burst out unexpectedly with a handful of men, catching the English off their guard and spiking some of the nearst siege guns. At the second time, he spotted Lord Grey de Wilton himself and accordingly rushed at him. The violence of his attack carried him right through to the English Commander, whom he knocked to the ground and nearly killed. Lord de Wilton's son, Arthur, ran to his father's assistance. For his filial devotion he also was felled with a blow to the shoulder from Bothwell's sword. Father and son were lucky to escape with their lives. The bemused guard finally rallied to their general: by force of numbers, Bothwell was obliged to return to the uncomfortable and doubtful security of the town walls. Behind him he left a carnage, to which his own men had also heavily contributed in dead and wounded.

But the situation inside the beleaguered town became increasingly difficult. Food was in very short supply. Rats spread disease. There was no way of replenishing ammunition. Despite all these troubles, morale remained high. When a major assault was finally launched by the English, the townsmen repulsed it with great loss to the attackers. They were considerably helped by the scaling ladders proving six feet too short. Also, there was a misunderstanding among the commanders. Two of the three principals thought the attack had been cancelled: the other went ahead on his own. One of the others joined in belatedly. The rebel contingent of Lord James Stewart stood by and did nothing.

Bothwell was not a man to stay immobilised in a besieged fortress. At nights he would slip out with parties of Borderers into the surrounding country and harry the outlying camps and supply depots of the English. He also conferred regularly with the Queen Dowager, who was sinking fast in the last stages of her disease. They had decided that he should make his way to France and try to raise help. A few days after the abortive attack on Leith, he went down to Crichton Castle, which had been patched up to a certain extent since its destruction by Lord James and Arran. Bothwell had lost a great number of his family possessions during the past few months. He had not spared his own resources in raising money and spending it on the Queen Dowager's behalf. These resources were now beginning to feel the strain of his loyalty. He had to sell land to maintain himself and his large body of retainers.

The Queen Dowager now sent him letters of recommendation to Frederik, King of Denmark, and to her daughter Mary, Queen of France. She also gave him instructions to see what help could be provided from any other source on the Continent. It was a last resort, but Bothwell threw himself into the important mission with his customary vigour.

After a round of visits to various people who had not declared themselves openly for the Lords, Bothwell left Scotland secretly in June. Cecil's spies reported that he had arrived at the Court of

Frederik II in Copenhagen. Frederik had a large and effective navy, which Bothwell doubtless thought would be useful in sweeping Admiral Winter and his ships from the Firth of Forth, thereby clearing the way for supplies to Leith. The visit seems to have been a great success. Bothwell was well able to match the King in his prodigious drinking and in many field sports. The King's favourite wineglass, which he used to offer to special guests, is still preserved in Copenhagen. It holds three litres. Bothwell was one of the few visitors who was able to drink it straight off on one occasion and still keep his place at the table.

But Bothwell did not delay long at the Danish Court after receiving promises of support from the King. As a mark of high honour, he was accompanied to the border of Germany by the King himself and his brother, the Duke of Holstein. In Germany, Bothwell had plans to raise five thousand mercenaries. If these could be obtained and ferried to Scotland in Frederik's navy, it would be a good prelude to a request to the French Court for massive aid.

Before he had time to negotiate for the mercenaries, the news came through to him that the Queen Dowager had died. Apart from his personal grief at the loss of someone for whom he had such great affection and respect, her death deprived him of his only influential ally and his staunchest supporter. The blow, although not unexpected, was stunning for him.

At one stroke, all his recent work counted for nothing. His high positions as confidant, adviser and Chief of Staff to the Head of State suddenly no longer existed. For at her death, there was no more reason for conflict between Scotland and England. Lord James Stewart and the Earl of Arran were now the natural leaders. Bothwell's and the Queen Dowager's struggles turned out to have been in vain. The siege of Leith was called off. Both sides had a picnic on the sands to celebrate the end of hostilities. A Treaty of Leith was drawn up and signed. With England no longer at loggerheads with the French, King Frederik of Denmark could not be expected to provide ships and men to support Bothwell alone. There was no further reason to raise mercenaries in Germany, and there was no further reason to seek aid from France.

Scotland would now be firmly in the Protestant hands of the rebel Lords, who would find no opposition. They lost little time in pursuing the few loyal followers of the dead Queen who had acted against them, despite the 'no victimisation' clause in the Treaty of Leith.

Bothwell was now on his own. It was a time for serious reflection. It was obvious that he would not be welcomed back to Scotland by Lord James Stewart and the rest of the rebels, now in the ascendant, and no longer 'rebels'.

During this period of bitter disappointment, when the beginnings of a great career had ended in nothing, he allowed himself a few weeks of idleness in which to take stock and plan a new future.

6

DURING HIS STAY in Copenhagen, Bothwell had been well entertained. Among those who had received him and his royal hosts, was a retired Norwegian admiral, Christian Throndssen. The Admiral had several unmarried daughters. The Scottish envoy not only cut a considerable dash, but also enjoyed the favour of the King. The Admiral thought one of his daughters would make a very suitable bride for the Earl. Chief candidate was Anna, with her jet black hair and good business head. Bothwell was accustomed to the attentions of women: he thought Anna pleasant enough, and did not discourage her. But Anna's parents were already thinking ahead. It was rumoured that their daughter would bring to any lucky husband of hers a dowry of forty thousand silver dollars. This rumour was current enough to be reported to Cecil back in England. He had been keeping a close watch on Bothwell's movements.

It would be uncharitable to suggest that such a handsome dowry would have influenced Bothwell's thoughts towards Anna. But the fact remained that he was very short of money, having spent so much of his own in the Queen Dowager's interest. It was not possible to sell more of his property to raise money while still on the Continent. To carry off his position and to maintain his entourage, while a guest of the King of Denmark, soon swallowed up what little money he had brought with him. Perhaps he could do worse than marry this apparently well-endowed girl, Anna Throndssen.

When he set off for Germany before the Queen Dowager's death, it is possible that he had either married Anna or promised that he would do so. Anna and her family claimed that he did marry her. The local records provide no adequate proof. Such evidence as exists is no more than hearsay or opinion. Throughout her long association with Bothwell, there is no record of her having described herself as Countess of Bothwell. It seems most likely that they were just good friends. Whatever the truth of it, the dowry of forty thousand dollars never materialised. Perhaps it had never existed. Anna insisted on accompanying Bothwell when he left Denmark. She was sufficiently taken up with him to sell all the jewellery and other possessions and give him the proceeds. For Bothwell was now without any resources at all, and quite unable to recoup his past expenses.

Anna had a kind heart, but she had some serious drawbacks. She was a self-opinionated and obstinate girl. Worse than this, she was an amateur poet, quite astonishingly devoid of talent, and had intellectual pretensions. This is evident in the various letters and poems she wrote to Bothwell during the next few years, many of which survive in copy or, occasionally, in original. Some of her effusions appear in that absurd hotchpotch of fact, forgery, and interpolation which came to be known as the Casket Letters. But whatever her failings, Anna was determined not to be left behind by the romantic Lord High Admiral of Scotland who had taken the social world of Copenhagen by storm. Having accepted her money, Bothwell was obliged to put up with her company, of which there is evidence he found tedious.

But on the news of the Queen Dowager's death, he realised he could not afford to dispense with the girl who was now his only means of financial support. It is clear that he explained his circumstances to her, told her that he had nothing substantial to offer her, and although very grateful to her for her help, suggested that she should return to her family.

Anna would not agree to leave him. She told him that she was now with child. She was certainly not going to be abandoned in that condition if she could help it. Bothwell had no option but to agree. There is no reliable record of where they spent the next few weeks. But by the middle of September, the English Ambassador in France reported to Cecil that Bothwell and Anna were in Flanders. They may have decided to settle down there. But a life of inactivity would not have suited Bothwell. In addition to this, he had promised the Queen Dowager to do what he could to help her daughter, Mary.

Bothwell was mindful of his promise. But the situation in Scotland was bound to be unfavourable to him, and he now had no money at all. There was only one thing to do. This was to go straight to the young Queen of Scots at her French Court, remind her of her mother's high opinion of him, and see whether he could not somehow be of service to her. A new life might await him at the French Court, or wherever Mary might wish to send him. Whatever she did, she would surely pay him. She might also refund him some, if not all, of his own money which he had spent in her mother's service.

This seemed an excellent plan. Bothwell explained it to Anna. There was one drawback; quite obviously, Anna could not accompany him. If he was to have the best chance of success, he must not be encumbered with a pregnant Norwegian girl. Never a master of subtlety, Bothwell doubtless explained this with little tact.

He brushed aside her objections. Wife or no wife, and pregnant or not, she was not coming with him. He might, he said, obtain a good position at the French Court, in which case he might send for her. Some years later, Anna claimed that Bothwell had taken her from her home and family under pretence of marriage, and abandoned her in Flanders. This was not true, since he returned to her after three monhs: Anna was glad enough to get what she could from him. It was she who abandoned him when he most needed her on a later occasion. When he lay in prison in a foreign country without friends to help him, Anna brought an action against him which effectively prevented his being released. Largely as a result of her action, he was never a free man again.

But now his mind was made up; he set out for the French Court to seek an audience of Mary Stuart, Queen of France.

The young King and Queen of France were at St Germain-en-Laye. Mary was ill and unable to receive anyone. She was now eighteen years old, unusually tall, with reddish hair and brown eyes. Her high colour and unnaturally clear skin were the result of various ailments with which she was born and from which she never recovered. Throughout her whole life she suffered from aches and pains, fits, bouts of uncontrollable weeping or laughter, and long periods of severe migraine. She was an undistinguished linguist, a faltering performer at song or musical instrument, and a horsewoman of no more than average ability. She had a chronic inability to make or take decisions. But to offset this modest catalogue, it was remarked on all sides that she had great presence and bearing. She had a personal charm, when she cared to exercise it, that captivated everyone. She was tenderhearted to a fault and deeply affectionate. She abhorred bloodshed and cruelty. And she had a sense of humour but not many occasions on which to practise it.

This was the young Queen of Scots upon whom her Lord High Admiral and Lieutenant of the Borders now waited.

But some time elapsed before Mary was well enough to receive him and the various other countrymen who had begun to congregate round her after her mother's death. It is not clear how he maintained himself during this awkward period. All Anna's goods and chattels had been sold. He could receive nothing from Scotland. And his own coffers were still empty. On the strength of his previous high position, and on the promise of paying back through sales of land on his return to Scotland, he probably borrowed money from merchants who knew him, or from friends who had also arrived at Court.

Apart from a later note by Mary saying that Bothwell had visited her, there is no surviving record of what transpired between them. He would have presented to her the recommendations he had received from her mother. Mary would probably have heard a lot about him from her. It is clear that he gave her a personal account of the situation in Scotland and pledged himself to carry out whatever orders or commissions might be entrusted to him.

According to the Treaty of Leith, signed after the Queen Dowager's death, a form of coalition government was to be set up in Edinburgh. This would be representative of the two main factions, the former rebel Lords and the followers of the late Queen. Bothwell offered to represent her in the organisation and establishment of this coalition: it is clear that Mary agreed with this course of action, and told him that she would appoint him in due course. There did not seem to be any special urgency about any of it. Mary now knew that she had a reliable representative, and that on the other side would be her half-brother, Lord James, of whom she was prepared to be quite fond. In her usual way of thinking that everyone always acted for the best motives, she visualised no difficulties of any sort. Everyone would now be friends, she was convinced, and everything would go happily on in peace and good order.

Unfortunately for Mary and all concerned, her interpretation of human nature was almost the opposite of reality. Lord James's brotherly love for Mary was less than skin-deep. From what he said and occasionally wrote, it is evident that he had made clear plans of how matters were to be arranged in Scotland. The coalition could be allowed to exist in theory, but in practice it was to be government by Lord James Stewart on behalf of his absent sister, Mary. She was to be kept absent. This would not be difficult, since she could not be expected to leave France as long as she remained Queen of France. When Elizabeth of England eventually died – she could be expected to live at least another thirty or forty years – then the situation could be reviewed. By that time, Lord James would be so firmly established, he thought, that he would be able to arrange matters to suit himself. He would anyhow be old enough to wish to retire, or appoint his own successor. Meanwhile Mary would be staying safely in France.

She quartered the arms of England with those of France, keeping alive her claim to succeed Elizabeth. This incensed the jealous Elizabeth and was never forgotten by her.

There then occurred most abruptly and unexpectedly an event which altered Mary's life completely. This was the death of her nineteen-year-old husband, Francis II, King of France. An abscess behind the ear developed suddenly as the Court was preparing to move to Orleans. Other complications arising from this caused his death within a few days. Bothwell had already left the Court. Mary was distraught, nursing the lad to whom she had been so devoted through his last agonies. Francis had never been physically strong. Like the rest of his family, he was completely dominated by his formidable mother, Catherine de Medici. It had not been expected that he would have a long life. A contemporary chronicle records that the marriage, as happy a one as was possible in the circumstances, had never been consummated. But the reliability of this information must be very dubious.

However, for Mary the light had gone out of her world. For a time, life itself appeared almost not to be worth living any more. Her own constitution was as frail as that of her husband: there were serious anxieties on her account. In addition to her grief at his loss, Mary now suffered the near hostility of her mother-in-law. Catherine de Medici had herself been deprived of the throne of France before due time by the sudden death of her husband, Henry, from his tournament accident. She had kept affairs very much in her own hands when her son Francis came to the throne. He was too young, trusting, and ill to wish to stand out against her, or to have many ideas of his own about the running of the country. She did not now propose to allow his widow to usurp her authority in any way, and pushed her next son, Charles, on to the throne with many instructions as to what he should do. Mary was immediately given to understand that she was to withdraw at once from public affairs. She could live quietly and obscurely in the depths of the country if she chose. Her allowance from the State as widow of the late King came to more than the whole revenue from Scotland, so she would always be well provided for. Alternatively, hinted the great Catherine, Mary might consider leaving the country altogether, which would be more satisfactory for all concerned, and take up her inheritance in Scotland.

Mary did not believe most of the stories Bothwell had told her about Scotland, about the treachery, feuding, fighting and mayhem which was Scotland's regular order of the day. If only she were to return, their own and rightful Queen of Scots, she thought, every man, woman and child would rally to her. She would bring peace and brotherly love to the whole country, and would reign in friendship and progress until the end of her days. The more she thought about the picture of her homeland, which she had painted for herself, the more she liked the idea.

During this period of indecision, envoys came direct from Scotland urging her to take this very course. There was no one at hand to give her warning. Bothwell had gone back to Flanders, to Anna Throndssen, and perhaps for the birth of a little boy called William. Scotland's principal Secretary and schemer, Maitland of Lethington, arrived with the warmest messages from her half-brother, Lord James Stewart. Would she return and rule? He would arrange all things for her and help her to rule the country. The next day another envoy arrived, representing those who had been loyal to the Queen Dowager. This was John Leslie, later Bishop of Ross. He in turn brought a message urging her to come back and take up where her mother had left off. Doubtless she would come with a new army of Frenchmen. They would sweep away the rebels once and for all, and Mary could become Queen of Scots indeed, with the whole country at her feet.

After the three months had elapsed during which these matters were being discussed, Bothwell returned to Scotland to give effect to the commission with which Mary had entrusted him. This was to get a Parliament summoned and the agreed coalition under way. She had given him summonses to three hundred of the people whom he had suggested to her would be most likely to be loyal. These were distributed by Bothwell in the name of the Queen, and the day for the meeting of Parliament duly arranged. He had evidently been given enough money by Mary to set himself up in reasonable conditions in Flanders, and to return to Scotland as a person of consequence. Anna travelled with him, but she is not described in the contemporary record as his wife, nor as the Countess of Bothwell. The child is not mentioned, although rumour had it that the child was born in Flanders, its impending arrival being the reason Bothwell did not travel directly home through Flanders after leaving the French Court.

The mystery about this child is as yet unsolved. It must have existed, since Bothwell's mother, the Lady of Morham, left all her belongings to it. But Bothwell himself is not recorded as ever having mentioned it. He makes no reference to it in the various statements and memoirs which he wrote. It is possible that at about this time in his career, he had a vision of himself as husband of Mary, Queen of Scots, with a son of theirs to succeed her on the throne. It would have been a fine thought. In such a dream, the lugubrious but too-faithful Anna could play no part. It would not be convenient at this stage to declare a son, or indeed admit to a marriage.

By all accounts, Bothwell settled her into one of his houses very comfortably. Nowhere has it been mentioned which was this house. The passport records show that, over the next few years, she made occasional journeys back and forth to Denmark from Scotland. But she was always Anna Throndssen and not the Countess of Bothwell.

He occupied this interval of time before Parliament was due to meet in a merry fashion. His chief activity was the arranging of a horse-racing match on the sands of Leith against Lord Ruthven. Both men had a very good eye for a horse and were skilled riders. Lord Ruthven had a very unattractive personality, and a reputation for callousness and cruelty, which he was to justify in due course in a chamber in Holyrood. But for the moment, his attention was on his horses. He kept a stud in England, where, he thought, the feed and grass were superior to those of the Edinburgh countryside. There were also better mares and stallions from which to choose. On this occasion, he sent down specially for several of his best geldings for the great match. Nothing of the match, of the race-card, of the distances or prizes unfortunately survives. The tradition of racing in the district is remembered today by the popular course at Musselburgh, adjoining the boundaries of Leith.

It is typical of Bothwell to have abandoned himself to a season's racing. He was able to forget that he was a controversial political figure, the leader of a faction with unrelenting enemies. Politics and diplomacy he evidently put out of his mind as he galloped about on the sands, trying one horse against another, discussing their merits and receiving reports about the likely performance of Lord Ruthven's geldings.

But there were others who used this period of waiting, almost of stagnation, to good purpose. Lord James Stewart and the hard core of his Lords were by no means inactive. He set himself to nullify the impression created in Mary's mind by Bothwell. Every skill of the wily Maitland of Lethington was used to convince the young Queen that Bothwell had grossly overstated the position. There was one person upon whom she could thoroughly rely. In addition to his great experience and knowledge of affairs, there was the tie of close relationship. She could safely and would wisely place her whole future in the hands of her loving half-brother, Lord James Stewart. She should come back at once, and give up all ideas of coalitions and suchlike. He would guide her in the way it was best for her to go.

Mary was in no position to assess what the real situation was. Lord James's ideas seemed very reasonable to her. She finally made the great decision. She would return to the Scotland she had left as a child of five, and her good half-brother would arrange everything suitably. Lord Bothwell would be there to help: had not her mother always said what a loyal servant he was? Mary had arranged that he should be given the guardianship of Dunbar Castle, which should keep him well satisfied, and close enough to Edinburgh should she need him. To stay in France would be altogether too difficult. Since she was Queen of Scots and no longer Queen of France, she might as well go to Scotland.

Plans began to be made for her journey. Her health being so unpredictable, it was decided that the Channel crossing from Calais would be the least taxing. The rest of the journey could be undertaken overland, with as many stops as might be needed to lessen the fatigue.

Application was accordingly made to London for a safe passage and permit to travel the length of England to the Scottish Border. To Mary's surprise, she was told that the granting of such permission was out of the question. Elizabeth did not feel secure enough on the throne to allow a royal progress throughout the country by her beautiful and captivating cousin. Successors to thrones often had ideas about succeeding earlier than might be the natural course. Besides, Mary was a figurehead of the Catholic Church. The north of England was still very largely true to the old religion: Henry VIII's Reformation to Protestantism had only a very tenuous hold. A journey such as Mary's might easily set the country in revolt against Elizabeth and her father's Reformation. In addition, there was the matter of Mary's quartering the English arms with her own.

Cecil was adamant. Elizabeth needed little persuading. Permission was refused. Cecil went further. Might it not be convenient if Mary fell into Elizabeth's hands before she even got to Scotland? This might easily be arranged and an adequate pretext concocted. The Lord James Stewart offered to obtain exact details of his dear half-sister's departure from France.

The offer was accepted. News came through to Mary that it would be wise to remove herself quickly and quietly, and that the long sea voyage was the only possibility. The person to arrange this was her Lord High Admiral of Scotland, the Earl of Bothwell. Sent for secretly and at once, Bothwell arrived in Paris on 5th July. It was impossible to do anything of this nature secretly in Paris, as others have found since that time. Sir Nicholas Throckmorton, Elizabeth's Ambassador to France, sent a note to Cecil the very day Bothwell reached the capital.

An effort had been made to camouflage Mary's movements. It was given out variously that she was not now going to Scotland, but staying in France; that she was travelling overland to Holland and embarking there; that she was too ill to move at all.

But Cecil was not deceived by any manœuvre. Bothwell could only have arrived and departed after three days for one reason. Throckmorton knew the reason well enough, although Mary herself denied it to him when he asked her outright what were her plans.

Bothwell had decided her best chance was in a small, fast ship, with two or three of the same as escort. It would not be so comfortable as the finest vessel offered by the new King of France. Charles had wanted to marry Mary himself, but his mother would not hear of it. The least he could do for her, in that case, was to provide a fine squadron to carry her to Scotland.

Bothwell may have thought that this would give to Elizabeth an excuse to make a large-scale naval attack, to declare that this was a French fleet threatening the English coast. But whatever the reason, he arranged for her transport to be lying ready at Calais on 14th August.

After taking nearly three weeks to come from Paris, Mary embarked and set sail. Hull-down in the Channel lay a squadron of Elizabeth's men-of-war. Cecil's information was as accurate as ever. It was only the heavy mist off the Goodwins which prevented their closing on the little contingent from Calais. As it was, they seized three ships, which went off course from the others. Two contained Mary's much-prized stud of horses. One contained Lord Eglinton. All were taken away. Lord Eglinton was later released in London, but the horses were never returned.

All the way up the east coast, Elizabeth's ships shadowed the poor Queen of Scots. Towards the end they began to close in. The Scots crammed on sail. But once more the heavy mists came rolling off the late summer swell. The Scottish ships vanished like wraiths along the inshore waters. Gaps in the watery horizon gave glimpses of the menacing English.

But Bothwell's sailors knew their job well. By luck and good seamanship, Mary's little party at last entered the Firth of Forth. It was 19th August 1561.

7

THE JOURNEY HAD proved too much for Mary. She took to her bed the day of her arrival. It was over two weeks before she emerged.

During that time, the many people who had declared that her coming would be Scotland's salvation and the means of unity, were deprived of showing their trump card, Mary herself. Had she been able to hold Court at once at Holyrood, to parade through Edinburgh, visit Stirling, start a progress through the surrounding country districts, there is no doubt she could have taken Scotland by storm. Her reign would at least have been launched on a wave of goodwill. Her bearing and charm, as well as her striking looks, all so approved by the people of France when she came to their throne, would undoubtedly have made it easier for her to establish herself with some authority. But with only rumour and second-hand stories to judge from, the personal impact she could have made was lost. The city had rapidly filled with people wishing to see her, greet her and do her homage. She was able to receive no one. Only priests were seen going in to her: this was an inauspicious start with the prevailing sensitivity about religion. Lord James Stewart, the Royal Bastard, also had an excellent opportunity of consolidating his position in her confidence, and of asserting his own influence over her. He was in constant attendance as she lay ill in her darkened room. Even had she been fit, she would not have been able to withstand such pressures. In her delicate condition, she wanted to do no more than agree with everything he suggested.

Lord James soon disposed of Bothwell, whom he had long

recognised as his chief opponent. Mary countermanded the gift of Dunbar Castle Keepership and transferred it to another illegitimate half-brother. The important Lieutenancy of the Border itself Mary agreed would be much better in Lord James's own hands. She also agreed that it was not politic, at this early stage in her reign, to risk any trouble between Bothwell and the near-lunatic Arran. Since Arran was so close to her in succession, it was desirable that he should be constantly at Court with her, at least as far as his failing wits would allow him. Bothwell had therefore better not come to Court for the time being. Mary again agreed. But she insisted on Bothwell being made – and remaining – a Privy Councillor.

Lord James had managed very well. He was in almost complete control. Mary would do whatever he said. Bothwell was safely out of the way and forbidden to come to the Court. Arran was as near mad as made no difference, and his father, the old Duke of Châtelherault, was too senile to be of any significance. The Earl of Morton, the head of the important Protestant Douglas family, was no danger. Provided Bothwell could be kept neutralised, Lord James saw an unlimited horizon ahead for his ambitions. As a tool for those machinations, he had Secretary Maitland of Lethington well under his control.

Mary soon realised the extent of her difficulties. Not only did she have to contend with bitter personal animosities among the influential nobles of the realm, she also had to suffer the raucous condemnations of John Knox, the Calvin-trained orator and self-appointed Messiah. Incited by him, there was almost a riot when Mary wished to hear Mass in her private chapel. This was especially discouraging for her, since one of her first declared intentions was to permit all forms of worship in the kingdom without hindrance. She had hoped that the same conditions might be applied to herself.

She was already heartily sick of the brawling and squabbling around her. When she finally got out and about in public, she found that most of the people had dispersed, and their potential goodwill towards her and each other and gone with them.

Mary was determined to do what she could to settle at least some of the hatreds and quarrels. Bothwell and Arran must be reconciled, she told Lord James. Was she already apprehensive and doubtful whether she could really trust those who pressed so close around her? Perhaps she had misgivings about the way Bothwell was kept away from her by Arran as well as Lord James. She had inadvertently intensified the Arran situation by granting the Abbey of Melrose to Bothwell, when it was already in Arran's keeping. She also told Lord James that she insisted he made up his own quarrel with Bothwell.

She gave instructions for them all to pay a visit to the Borders at Berwick, the country she had heard so much about from Bothwell, and also from her mother. It appears that she was already beginning to feel the lack of Bothwell's association, even if she had only enjoyed it on odd occasions up until now. This expedition might pave the way for his admittance to Court again by Lord James, Arran and the rest.

Mary may have felt that too much was being done to keep Bothwell out of her way, and was beginning to wonder why. In the Borders, Bothwell would be very much on his own ground and would not be likely to come to harm, nor to provoke anyone else, especially if the whole idea had been that of Mary herself. This seemed a good way of getting all these quarrelsome people together at last, people who should all be working in unity for her and for Scotland.

There was general agreement about the progress, which was to be a goodwill visit to Berwick in the name of the Queen.

It was a success from the point of view of reconciliations. Lord James and Bothwell gave a good impression of friendship, and both were well received and entertained at Berwick. Visits to Seton, just outside Edinburgh, and a night at Dunbar, on the way down, had gone off without incident. If there was any difficulty at Dunbar Castle, so recently promised to Bothwell and taken away again for Lord James, there is no record of it.

They stayed at Coldinghame on the return journey. The Commendator, or lay Keeper of Coldinghame Abbey, was one of Lord James's half-brothers, Lord John Stewart. perhaps the most sympathetic of the bastard trio. He took a great fancy to Bothwell's sister, Janet, who had been travelling with the party. The likelihood of this relationship being carried further was a good omen for the future good relationship between Bothwell and Lord James. The Queen was especially happy when this likelihood was reported to her. She was already fond of Janet Hepburn and probably more fond of Lord John than of Lord James.

All this led to a general improvement in atmosphere and feeling. Mary was delighted at the apparent success of her campaign. In November Bothwell came to Court to sign a document of continued friendship towards anyone considered to be an opponent of him or his family. It was unfortunate that the friendship treaty was limited to a duration of only three months, but it was better than no treaty at all.

In continuation of this new amity, Bothwell went down again to the Borders in company with Lord James and the Earl of Morton to carry out a round of judicial duties. Bothwell's feelings, as the former Lieutenant of the Borders, can be imagined while Lord James, the new Lieutenant, conducted affairs.

Lord James was a man of little compassion. He preferred to hang or drown nearly everyone brought before him, whether man, woman or child. While Bothwell had been vigorous in pursuing offenders and having them arraigned, there are many records of his clemency. He had discovered that firmness, tempered with occasional leniency, was the best formula for keeping the peace in those naturally lawless communities.

Bothwell and Lord James soon returned to Edinburgh. During their absence, the Duke of Châtelherault and his son, Arran, together with other Protestant Lords and prominent members of the former 'Rebels', had been taking stock of their position in Mary's eyes. It was evident to them that Mary did mean what she said; she did not intend any religious persecution or attempts to banish former disloyal elements. Encouraged by this, they came forward openly to her Court. As was to be expected, she received them with assurances of goodwill and repeated her hopes that everyone would live in amity together.

Bothwell was anxious to fall in with her plans. But according to detailed information sent by the spy Randolph to Cecil, the source of most of the fact and gossip at this time, the general goodwill did not extend from the Hamiltons to Bothwell. Perhaps Bothwell was already showing signs of over-confidence in his championship of the Queen. For when the old Duke, head of the Hamilton family, told the Queen that he was making arrangements to be present at the Annual Church Assembly that winter, it was Bothwell who expressed pleasure in a regal way, and gave the Duke an undertaking of friendship and an assurance of his safety. This was more than the Duke could take, especially since he considered the Hamiltons to be infinitely superior to the Hepburns, and Bothwell himself to be a man of no particular position attempting to ingratiate himself with the Queen.

Instead of receiving Bothwell's messages with mild dignity, which would have been the most effective way, he sent back a crushing reply. Who on earth was Bothwell, he said, to offer or guarantee anything to one such as himself? He was well able to look after himself, and would be obliged if Bothwell would keep such impudent approaches for those more suited to his modest rank. Randolph was delighted to be able to report Bothwell's discomfiture to Cecil. His master was probably also well satisfied at this evidence of how the chief enemy of England's interests in Scotland had been so firmly put in his place.

Bothwell took care that Mary should learn of his rebuff. She urged him not to react, and to bear in mind her great anxiety that there should be no strife. This is one of the occasions which show that Mary and Bothwell, even at this stage, were in the habit of exchanging opinions on comparatively minor matters. The majority of those around her appeared chiefly to discuss matters concerning the affairs of the country. But with Bothwell the subjects were often more personal. The keen ear of Randolph picked these up whenever possible. Cecil knew of them all within a few days.

As for the Duke's response, Bothwell agreed to let it pass. But he did not see why the Duke's son Arran, who had always caused Bothwell so much trouble, should share his father's immunity. Randolph again records the details. It came to Bothwell's notice that Arran was increasingly often to be found of an evening at the house of a young married lady called Alison Craig. Alison was evidently a sociable girl and had many friends. She was the daughter-in-law of the same Bishop of Durham who had represented the English at the Border Conference the year before, and had insisted on holding the meetings in the middle of the Tweed. The Bishop was a man of parts: he was the Cuthbert Tunstall whom Bothwell's grandmother had once married as her fourth husband. Arran was not the only one to enjoy Alison's hospitality on occasion. Rumour had it that Bothwell himself was sometimes to be found paying her a visit.

With a certain lack of chivalry, perhaps tinged with jealousy, Bothwell and a few friends, including the Marquis d'Elboeuf and Lord John Stewart of Coldinghame, now his sister's fiancé, made a boisterous raid on poor Alison's convivial home. It was Christmas 1561, and there was much carousing in the streets of Edinburgh. The idea was to burst in upon Arran and to discredit him in a lighthearted fashion on being discovered accepting the hospitality of such a well-known hostess.

But Arran was not there, so Bothwell and his friends were merely made to look fools themselves. Instead of letting the matter go at that, Bothwell insisted on trying again the next night. This time Arran was indeed there, but got out by the back way at the first sign of company. Hot on the scent, Bothwell and his cronies broke down hurriedly bolted doors and searched the house. Like so many jokes, it had gone too far. It was now a case of frightening a citizen at night, breaking in and damaging her property. Formal complaint was made to the Queen and once more Bothwell was made to look very stupid as his plan backfired.

The story received wide currency. The second stage of it was even recorded by Philip of Spain's Ambassador in his official dispatches to Madrid. Diplomatic affairs must have been in the doldrums for details of such an escapade to occupy the time of foreign ambassadors. Da Quadra, the Spanish Ambassador, reported that Mary had reprimanded Bothwell and his merrymakers, made excuses for them on all sides, and trusted that the matter could now be forgotten.

But the Hamiltons were not a family to be made fun of without wishing to have the last word. Very shortly afterwards, on Christmas Eve itself, three hundred of them, including many general retainers and supporters, resolved to teach Bothwell a hearty lesson for his impudence. Filling the dark alleyways along which Bothwell would be returning from a dinner party, they lay in wait soon after dark. But Bothwell was not to be caught as easily as that. He never went to the dinner. With a rare stroke of prudence, he ensured that the Queen got to know that he had been threatened with violence by the Hamiltons. He realised well enough that he would otherwise have been blamed for starting any trouble which might follow.

In a very short time he raised nearly five hundred of his own supporters. The streets and taverns were full of men owing allegiance to every nobleman in the place, all full of ale and their spirits high after days of roistering. It would be a matter of minutes, in those congested and festive conditions, for anyone to rally all his supporters and friends, if there looked like being a little trouble.

Very soon it became apparent that there was going to be a serious clash in the centre of the city. No one would be able to resist joining in, on one side or the other. Edinburgh would be in uproar if nothing was done about it. Fortunately, the city authorities and the palace guard from Holyrood had been alerted by Bothwell's message. Before weapons could be drawn, order was restored and everyone sent off the streets. But it was a near thing. Mary was furious that such riotous conduct had broken out so soon after everyone had promised to be on their best behaviour. And on Christmas Day, too.

The Hamiltons indignantly denied any responsibility. The Duke protested most vigorously at the suggestion that he or his son could possibly be involved in a common brawl in the streets. It was all the doing of a young Hamilton called Gavin, who had merely wished to protect the honour of the Earl of Arran, which had been so assailed by Bothwell the day before. The Duke told the Queen that nothing would induce him to discuss anything with Bothwell, in order to resolve the matter, unless Bothwell publicly retracted the monstrous charges of conspiracy against the Hamiltons.

Bothwell would certainly not do this. Randolph again reported gleefully, and in detail, that the Queen then decided that the only alternative was for Bothwell to leave Edinburgh at once. She knew he would loyally obey her. It was certainly easier to dismiss him with this knowledge, than to try it on the Hamiltons, with their long record of antagonism against her mother. It might need little to rekindle such antagonism. So Bothwell was ordered to leave. And he left, as Mary knew he would.

He went straight to Crichton to get ready for his sister Janet's wedding to Lord John Stewart in a couple of weeks' time.

Mary had promised she would come to the wedding, and stay at Crichton the night. This latest bout of unruliness in Edinburgh had not affected her promise.

She went to Crichton for the occasion. She had given Janet a fine length of silver brocade and other presents. It was altogether a splendid, but expensive, day. Bothwell could count many very satisfactory features to offset the huge cost of it all. The Queen had come to the wedding, had stayed the night in his house, and one of the principal guests had been Lord James Stewart, a long-established rival and a dangerous, if temporarily quiescent, enemy. These were important things in Bothwell's life. He would have reckoned them worth the enormous banquet he had to give, the refurbishing of the castle to receive the Queen and all the guests, the new clothes and tidy harness his retainers and their horses would have to wear. Also the organisation of all the games, dancing and competitions at the celebrations afterwards. Even the decoration of the chapel had been expensive, since the Queen had come to the ceremony as well, although it had been a Protestant service.

It really looked as if things would quieten down now. When the Queen left Crichton the next day with Lord James and some of the others, Bothwell would doubtless have felt quite pleased with himself and optimistic for the future.

8

AFTER RETURNING TO Edinburgh, Mary was more determined than ever to consolidate the progress of her campaign for universal friendship. Lord James and Bothwell were now getting on well enough, she thought, after the pleasant couple of days together at Crichton. The wedding had also created an additional family link that might hold them together. Her optimism again won the day. Family links are not always a sure bond, as she was to discover. The only outstanding disagreement that still mattered was between Bothwell and the Earl of Arran. Bothwell told her again that he was quite willing to be friends, despite his previous unsuccessful attempts in this direction. Let Arran come and sign a document saying that he was also willing.

This seemed reasonable enough. Mary sent word to Arran that she would like him to come and do this. To begin with, nothing would induce Arran to take this step. He was afraid of plots and trickery on Bothwell's side, he told the Queen: if Bothwell wanted to be friends, there was nothing to prevent him. Why should he, the most peaceable man you could find, be obliged to sign agreements with a proved troublemaker such as that wild man Bothwell? But unlike the occasion when Arran's father had received Bothwell's assurances of goodwill, this time Mary was convinced that Bothwell was being most reasonable, and Arran merely recalcitrant. Her sudden temper alarmed Arran. It did not take much to alarm him, but contemporary accounts suggest that Mary's temper could alarm more resolute characters than his. Randolph reported that Arran hurried round to Holyrood to sign whatever document was placed before him. The Register of the

Privy Council for the 20th February 1563 shows that the Queen summoned him before it, although he complained of being too ill to appear. The wavering signature was fully witnessed: the names of Lord James and Cockburn of Ormiston were added, together with that of Bothwell. Mary congratulated everyone concerned on having taken such an important and useful step.

But Bothwell had signed only in order to please the Queen. He knew as well as anybody that Arran was capable of signing any document without allowing it to influence his subsequent actions. The only hope of keeping Arran from plotting was to get closer to him, to convince him that he was himself in no danger from anything Bothwell might do. Bothwell resolved to find an intermediary whom Arran could be expected to trust, and try to arrange a meeting.

John Knox seemed the best person to try. Bothwell had little time for his hypocritical ranting, and had never been a close acquaintance. But he had seen more of Knox since the Queen's arrival in Scotland, and had been present on one occasion when the preacher's bullying had reduced her to tears.

He went to see Knox, as privately as he could, in the galleried house overlooking the High Street. An old house is pointed out to this day as the one which might have been his. Knox was apprehensive, but agreed to do what he could as intermediary. Bothwell then set off for Berwick, where he was to take part in one of the innumerable litigations concerning the town's relations with the neighbouring countryside.

He nearly lost his life on the journey down. For he unexpectedly came upon Alexander Cockburn of Ormiston, young son of the Cockburn whom Bothwell had relieved of the English gold destined for Lord James's forces. Randolph records, seemingly regretfully, that when young Alexander, on the impulse, pulled a pistol on his father's ill-user and fired it point blank into his face, it failed to go off. It would have been the end of Bothwell. It would also have been the end of young Sandy, and probably of the rest of the Ormiston family, within a very short time.

But Bothwell seemed unperturbed. He had Alexander seized and taken along with them, but did nothing more about it. He probably felt that this was not the moment for violence, whatever the provocation, when he was hoping for peaceful reconciliations with his adversaries. The Ormistons could be dealt with any time it was necessary. When he got to Berwick, Bothwell had Alexander sent home unharmed. The young Ormiston was lucky.

But Knox heard about the incident, possibly from Randolph, who told him that it was Bothwell who had made an unprovoked attack on the Ormistons, father and son. Only when further evidence reached him that Randolph once more had been trying to get Bothwell into more trouble than he usually found for himself, did Knox agree to continue his efforts to bring Arran and Bothwell together.

In this good office he eventually succeeded. The meeting was arranged to take place in the Hamilton town house. Knox reported the details in full: he saw himself in the role of peacemaker and true Christian, and did not wish his leading part in the affair to be overlooked.

When Bothwell came in, Arran 'gently passed unto him, embraced him, and said: "If the hearts be upright, few ceremonies will serve" .' The two of them then spoke privately together for some little while. No record exists of what they said. Bothwell was no diarist, and Arran was in no condition to sit down calmly and enter up the day's events in a journal. In view of what Arran immediately afterwards alleged had passed between them, it seems that their talk may have been more than a mere exchange of pleasantries. It is, however, not likely that Bothwell would have broached to Arran at that moment a plan for a serious plot against the Queen. He had had no contact with Arran beforehand, as far as is known, and had no means of knowing even how he would be received. If there was any plot, this does not seem to have been a good moment to put it forward.

They certainly kept close company for the next three days. People were astonished to see such well-known adversaries going about together as if they had been friends all their lives. They dined together, went on a sporting expedition together, even went over to visit Arran's father, the old Duke of Châtelherault, at Kinniel, where they were entertained.

But on the fourth day, an amazing thing happened. Knox and Randolph, close chroniclers of these matters, recorded the facts of it.

Arran appeared to have some sort of brainstorm. He rushed

64

round to Knox and poured out an extraordinary story. He said that Bothwell had made him party to a plot to kill Lord James Stewart and Secretary Lethington, and to abduct the Queen. It had been arranged, he swore, that Mary should be taken to the Hamilton fortress of Dumbarton, and that he, Arran, should take over the country and rule with Mary. Increasingly distraught, Arran went over the so-called plot again and again, waving aside Knox's incredulous questions and attempts to calm him down.

Without producing any evidence of his story, Arran then rushed out into the street and back to the Hamilton house. From here he sent a messenger to the Queen and Lord James with the whole story repeated and elaborated. Mary was at that moment at Falkland Palace, twenty miles north of Edinburgh in Fife, and the favourite centre for hunting and hawking. The tale now included such details as Bothwell's assurance to Arran that he could arrange for Mary to marry him, and had ample reserves of men to carry the plan through by force if necessary. Bothwell himself had promised that nothing and nobody would be allowed to stand in the way.

The amazing news was given to the Queen and Lord James while they were out hunting. Mary was evidently very astonished and inclined to disbelieve it. But Lord James was not so surprised. Knox had told him before, as he himself records in his history, that Arran was becoming a prey to the most absurd beliefs and was liable to say or do almost anything. Knox had urged Lord James to pay no attention to any story that might reach him from Arran. And now, here was just such a story.

But for Lord James it was a very convenient story, even a little too convenient to be accepted four centuries later, when so much additional information about it cannot be produced. Here was an excellent and final means of doing away with Arran under charge of complicity in treason. Arran was still the best claimant to the throne after Mary, and might still manage to get himself married to her. Arran remained Lord James's biggest rival for power, despite his increasing madness. Lord James accordingly issued orders at once for Arran's immediate detention in the name of the Queen. Mary was scarcely consulted. As for Bothwell, Lord James now had a perfect excuse to get him thrown into prison with every prospect of his only way out being to the scaffold. He would be taken in the very act of plotting treason and worse. The order went out to arrest him, too.

Arran's mind was now disintegrating fast. He galloped like the mad thing he was from Edinburgh to his father's house at Kinniel, some seven or eight miles away. The old Duke and his household wearily received the dishevelled creature and locked him up. This was not the first time this sort of thing had happened to his son and heir. In fact, the Duke was reported to have said 'twice before, he was in the same case', and then to have added quickly, and a little smugly: 'He takes it of his mother.' The Duke urged Mary to forget the whole incident. Mary probably would have been glad enough to do so. But Lord James was not going to give up such opportunities for clearing the field of his rivals.

The mad Earl escaped from his father's custody, but not before he had sent off yet another letter. This time it was to Lord James, giving the information that it was his own father, the poor Duke, who was behind the plot. Lord James knew this to be nonsense, but did not say so. The more the Hamiltons were involved in scandal or disgrace, the better for him.

Arran arrived in the middle of the night at the house of the soldier Kirkcaldy of Grange. Grange was appalled by all the conflicting and garbled stories produced by Arran. He sent at once to Lord James to say Arran was with him. Although mostly out of his mind, Arran had brief periods of sanity. One of these coincided with Lord James's arrival at the house. Arran promptly denied all the stories, messages and letters he had sent out. His father had nothing to do with any of it. There were no plots by anyone. He could not think what had come over him. Lord James hurriedly silenced him before such a complete retraction could spoil everything. Arran was hustled away to St Andrews after a brief questioning, and later to Edinburgh. By January 1564, Randolph was reporting to Cecil that Arran was permanently mad, ill of all sorts of diseases including jaundice, and kept chained up in a dark cell. In 1566, according to Randolph, he was let out on bail put up by his former friends and kept under restraint, but not in prison. Incredibly, he survived for another forty-three years.

On the day that Arran's first letter reached the Queen and Lord

James, Bothwell arrived all unsuspecting at Falkland. Had there been the slightest truth in any of Arran's charges against him, he would hardly have ridden in so freely. To his astonishment, he was at once arrested and charged with treason. Arran was made by Lord James to repeat everything to his face in the presence of the Queen and the Privy Council. By this time Arran was prepared to say anything. Bothwell most strongly denied everything and issued a challenge to Arran, having no other way of defending himself. He demanded a proper trial, but no one would listen to him, not even the Queen. He also was hurried away to the prison in St Andrews.

After some ten or twelve weeks there without opportunity of getting a trial, he was transferred to the greater security of a cell in Edinburgh Castle.

Here, many people campaigned on his behalf in an effort to help him get a proper trial. Intercessions to the Queen were always blocked by Lord James, who was now in complete control. Mary had let things get so far that she was now powerless to restrain her half-brother. He did exactly as he pleased; she was obliged to sign whatever documents he laid before her. She had no champion, and no one to stand up for her.

For Lord James, the tide was running strongly. His rival, Arran, was now safely out of the way for all time. His dangerous adversary, Bothwell, was in the securest prison in the country, in the heart of Edinburgh, and had been put there by command of the Privy Council and of the Queen herself. Prisoners did not normally last very long in Edinburgh Castle: there was no reason why Bothwell should be an exception.

One trouble spot remained. This was the Gordon family, Earls of Huntly, known as Cock of the North for swinging from one side to another with the irregularity of a weathercock. They were big landowners and could raise a sizable army of their own. In addition, they were staunch Catholics, leaders of the faith in the north-east. These were the only people left who might wish to challenge Lord James. They might also be able to get the support of the Queen if any rift came between her and him. With his customary ruthless planning, Lord James decided that all the Gordons should be eliminated. It was not difficult to let the Gordons think that a Catholic rising for the Catholic Queen against her Protestant advisers might have a very good chance of success. Two of the Earl of Huntly's sons, the Earl himself, and several of his relations, considered the matter carefully.

They had strong support in their part of Scotland, which was most of the north-east centred on Aberdeen. The chances looked good, and the rising began to take shape. In triumph, Lord James laid the latest reports before the Queen. It was imperative for her to make a progress to the north and sweep all such dangerous insurrection and disloyalty away.

Mary hated any suggestion of bloodshed. But if she went up herself, she thought, with a large force led by her loving half-brother, Lord James, all opposition would surely crumble without violence, and all who felt disaffected would from that moment bind themselves loyally to her. She therefore agreed to a military progress. In August 1562, she set off with Lord James, who had now become the Earl of Mar, a dignity more in keeping, he thought, with his new position as executive head of State.

Back in his Edinburgh cell, Bothwell took stock of his career, which seemed to have ended so abruptly and unfairly. Surely the Queen knew he would never have been party to anything so treacherous and unlikely as the scheme suggested by the mad Arran? Surely she did not really wish him to spend the rest of his days in a prison? It was too improbable to be true. But what did she really think?

Bothwell describes in his own rather abbreviated memoirs the way these thoughts came to his mind, and how he determined to get from the Queen herself what her thoughts were about him. Either by letter or word of mouth, he arranged for his questions to be brought to the Queen while she was still on her northern progress. His detention may not have been as severe as was customary in the castle. But Bothwell was a popular figure up to that time. Lord James could never lay claim to popularity, but there is no evidence that this caused him any loss of sleep. The Queen's message in reply soon came back to Bothwell. 'I discovered,' he wrote in French, 'that she knew well enough that I had only been accused through motives of personal hatred and envy, but that, for the time being, she was quite unable to give me any help or assistance, since she virtually wielded no authority at all. But she sent a message to say that I was to do the best I could for myself——.'

He then adds, without further ado: 'Because of this reply, I made every effort to get out of prison.'

His first effort succeeded. It is not clear how much inside help he received. Knox declared that as soon as the Queen's reply became known, he walked out through the front gate to freedom. If this had been the case, it seems certain that Cecil's informants would have got wind of it and reported it to him. But their impression is that he forced a bar from his window on the particularly stormy night of 28th August and got away down the rocky cliff upon which the castle is perched. He is known to have been helped by the Castle Keeper's personal servant, James Porterfield, who appears again later in the story. Bothwell certainly had friends to help him get away. It is probable that he chose to go down the cliff, rather than through the gate, in order not to incriminate any servant or official in the prison.

Once free, he made his way to Morham, where his mother received him. From there he went to Crichton Castle and in no way acted as a fugitive. No one seems to have taken any steps to recapture the escaped prisoner. From here he went on down to the Hermitage. He found the great castle in good order, well stocked and provisioned for his occupation, all of which had been done entirely at the expense of the much maligned Lady Janet Scott, the Lady of Branxholm. It was not the first, nor the last, good deed she did him.

He felt safe enough here to write to the Queen explaining that he had indeed 'done the best he could for himself' and would now be glad to place himself entirely at her service. He wrote at the same time to Lord James, Earl of Mar. He also sent a note to Secretary Lethington offering his friendship and inviting him to help smooth his path towards a return to favour. Mary had stayed at Spynie with the old Bishop of Moray, Bothwell's guardian in his youth and his lifelong friend.

It is likely that no letter reached the Queen which had not already passed through Lord James's hands. Many letters and general communications, therefore, never reached her at all. There is no evidence that she received this letter of Bothwell's, since no reactions are recorded. This would be very unusual for Mary.

Bothwell not only received no encouragement from any of these quarters, but he received no replies at all, as we learn from the dispatches of Cecil, who was taking a keen interest in the new turn of events. Sir John Forster, English Warden of the Borders, reported to Cecil that Bothwell was behaving most peaceably and sensibly, and that everything was quiet around him. Bothwell evidently hoped to show by this attitude that the Queen could safely readmit him to her Court, and that he planned no violence or vengeance to anyone as a result of his imprisonment.

But Lord James, furious at Bothwell's escape, was certainly not going to allow him to return to the Queen's favour and public life, if he could help it. He would deal with Bothwell when the royal progress was completed. It had been very satisfactory up to the moment. A lot of repression had been carried out by Lord James, in the reluctant Queen's name, with great severity. Moreover, it looked as if the Earl of Huntly and his family would soon be provoked into open battle, and consequently annihilated.

This is what did occur, at the one-sided affray known as the Battle of Corrichie. The Gordons had no intention of such an engagement, but were tricked into it. The Earl was killed with many of his family, clan, and supporters, quite unnecessarily from the Queen's point of view. The Earl's young son was ceremoniously hanged, an occasion which the Queen refused to attend, despite Lord James's pressing invitation. All the Huntly property was confiscated. Lord James concluded the whole campaign by taking for himself a large amount of goods and property. He then suggested to the Queen that she now create him Earl of Moray. To no one's surprise, she acceded to his request. Lord James was known from then on as Moray. His cup of ambition and greed began to flow over.

Bothwell did not fit anywhere into Moray's detailed plans for the future. As soon as he returned from the campaign, he issued instructions for Bothwell to surrender himself at once under penalty of indictment for treason. Mary herself had taken to her bed after the rigours and violence of the campaign, all of which had turned out so different from what she had hoped. She could do nothing about Bothwell, or indeed about any of the things in which she would have liked to have played an important part. She was reported to have sunk thankfully on to her cushions and instructed the blinds to be drawn. This was partially to relieve her appalling headaches. It was probably also a symbolic withdrawal from the turbulence in her life which she so much detested. She would have liked to have helped Bothwell, to have tried again for general conciliations all round, to have established a peaceful régime. But the effort was too much. For a fortnight again she stayed in her darkened room. Moray made the most of it.

For Bothwell, things were once more looking difficult. He had not been able to look after his affairs properly. He had to raise money wherever he could, mostly by sale and mortgage, to keep himself and his establishments going. It seemed that his life was in danger once more. Moray would certainly get him into prison again, and the Queen was too ill to do anything about it. The only consolation was that he now knew Mary would have done something had she been physically capable of it.

Moray now put it around that Bothwell was to be arrested. Time was short. So was money. There seemed nothing for Bothwell to do but leave the country again and go over to France, where he knew he had some good friends.

Randolph reported that he had paid a quick visit to Leith, surrounded by hard-riding, heavily-armed Borderers. No one would go through to Leith unless they were interested in ships. Cecil had the port watched, but Bothwell was also having the port watched. Either by chance or by arrangement, ten local merchants had chartered a small vessel to trade to France some time during December. Although the names of the merchants survive, the date of their departure is not recorded. But on that little ship as she fell away down the tide to France, stood the lonely figure of the Earl of Bothwell. As she heeled and dipped to the heavy sea which rose that night, he must have reflected on what were the wages for loyalty and service to a sovereign.

He could have spared himself the trouble of a secret departure. Little, if anything, was secret to Cecil's spies. The instant a watcher at Leith had reported the departure of the ship with its distinguished passenger, a rider left for London. By pre-arrangement the coast was to be watched if Bothwell left by sea. All Edinburgh knew at once that he had gone. Many thought it would be for the last time. Moray sent out orders for the surrender of the Hermitage and the forfeiture of other property.

Whatever was in Bothwell's mind as the ship plunged along the coast in increasingly bad weather, he could not have anticipated what actually happened. The vessel had to run for shelter into the little harbour at Holy Island in Northumberland. Bothwell went ashore with the one servant who had accompanied him from Leith. Together they set out on foot, through the handful of houses which make up the high-tide island village, and across the three-mile stretch of sand, laid bare at low tide, to the mainland. From here, legend and tradition combine to provide the only evidence that Bothwell made his way the ten miles to Coldinghame, home of his sister Janet and her husband, Lord John Stewart. All records are blank for the next few days, but there is no reason to doubt the legend.

For who should arrive at Coldinghame within the next two days and stay until the end of the week, but the Queen herself? This time she had escaped fron Moray's clutches: she arrived with the merest handful of attendants and a few heavily-armed mounted bodyguards.

It is not surprising that no official record exists of what happened during the four days after Mary had arrived. It can well be imagined what discussions took place, what plans were made.

But whatever was decided, on the next Sunday, Bothwell's man, William Tatt, rode into the village of Berrington, four miles over the Border into Northumberland, in company with a local man, whose name is not recorded. Together they came to the house of a man call John Rively. Arrangements were made for a small barn near the house to be made available for a few days for Tatt's master. It is not clear whether Rively knew in the first instance who his guest was to be. The barn was a particularly secure building with what appeared to be a stone roof, the whole possibly built in a cleft in the rock, or even a large cave provided with firmly locking doors. A close study of the modern hamlet of Berrington has not revealed any natural feature which could readily fit the contemporary description. Yet it must have been of some size. For on the next day, Bothwell rode up accompanied by the Edinburgh lawyer, David Chalmers, and the same James Porterfield who had helped him escape from Edinburgh Castle. And all the men, together with their horses, went safely inside the building and the door was locked.

This seemed an admirable shelter from which to arrange for a further passage by ship to continue the journey to France.

But although the delay since arrival at Holy Island had not been long, it had been long enough for the news to reach Randolph, the spy in Edinburgh. Randolph had a fixation about Bothwell, perhaps stimulated by handsome payments from Cecil. But his assiduous tracking and reporting of Bothwell seems on occasion to have been beyond the call of duty. Today, however, duty called firmly. Randolph advised the commander of the Garrison Guard at Berwick, Captain Carew, that the ship carrying a person fleeing from an order to return to prison in Scotland had put into Holy Island. Would he please detain and search the ship, and if possible, arrest the fugitive Earl of Bothwell?

The details of what happened next appear in the local historical record, some fact, some not. But there seems no reason to doubt it, since there would be little point in making it up.

On the very day that Captain Carew was making a detailed search of the few houses which make up the village of Holy Island, John Rively's nephew was buying a bottle of wine with which his uncle wished to entertain his clandestine visitor. Wine would naturally be more readily available at the small seaport than in any of the inland villages. Not unnaturally, the nephew was noticed and recognised. Instead of following him, Captain Carew went back to Berwick. That evening, it seems that the Captain made contact most secretly with John Rively. For whatever happened during the evening at Rively's house, Bothwell began to suspect that there was danger. On going to the stone-roofed shelter for the night, Bothwell lay down without undressing. He had given instructions for two of the party also not to undress, but to stay fully clothed near the door, their weapons within easy reach. All the horses were to be saddled and bridled, and to remain so all night. After seeing his orders carried out, Bothwell went to sleep.

In the early hours of the next morning, while it was still pitch dark, a strong force from the garrison at Berwick came quietly up to Rively's house, under the command of the Under-Marshal, the Master of the Ordnance, and Captain Carew. Rively at once woke up and went to the door himself, probably an unusual thing to do. Without apparently showing surprise or having any discussion, he took the officers and their men straight across to the locked doors of Bothwell's building.

With supreme treachery, Rively is on record as having shouted through the heavy doors that there were friends of the Lord Bothwell's just arrived, who wished to speak to him. The men unbolted the door. The garrison rushed in and secured everyone inside in a matter of moments.

Rively is noted as having stood well clear when Bothwell was brought out. He was wise. The Earl of Bedford, later governor of Berwick, writing to Cecil some time afterwards, reported that Bothwell had declared 'he meant not to kill any in England so soon as Cecil and one Rively'.

Bothwell was taken straight to Berwick and put in the Castle prison. Rively also was placed under arrest, possibly to save him and his family from vengeful action by any of Bothwell's supporters, had the extent of his betrayal of a trusting guest ever been suspected. By being arrested, he would be made to appear innocent of any treachery. He was soon released on bail. He then went down to see Cecil himself, a difficult journey to explain for those who wished to clear the name of Rively.

9

THE WARDEN OF BERWICK, Sir Thomas Dacre, was not overjoyed at the prospect of keeping the former Lieutenant of the Borders a prisoner under his charge. In the first place, it was not clear what crime Bothwell had committed to justify his detention in England. Secondly, Berwick was not very far from the centre of Bothwell's home ground. Sir Thomas had already suffered from contact with the Hepburns in former days. He did not relish the idea of becoming known as the gaoler of the Earl of Bothwell. He accordingly gave his prisoner every facility to alter the situation.

This Bothwell did by writing to his old adversary, the Earl of Northumberland, who at that time was at Elizabeth's Court in London. His letter survives. It is a brief and dignified protest about his treatment, and a request to a former honoured opponent to put in a good word for him with Queen Elizabeth.

Bothwell thought that Moray would do all he could to get him sent back to Scotland. Some charge of treason would then be trumped up, and he would either lose his life or spend the rest of it in prison again. He could not look to Mary for more than goodwill, which would not turn prison locks. It therefore seemed safer to stay in England. But not in a gaol. If his old adversary could use his influence at Court, perhaps they could become comrades. Perhaps Queen Elizabeth would care to give him some responsible post until matters improved and he could safely return to Scotland. 'I would,' he suggested to Northumberland, '. . . offer her my humble service personally.'

Cecil was in favour of returning him to Scotland to certain imprisonment. Once in Moray's hands, he thought, no one could last long. But Moray was of the opinion that Bothwell would be better kept in England. He was a constant anxiety in Scotland. No prison seemed to be secure enough to keep him. Mary would never allow him to be executed: this was one thing about which Moray could not guarantee to persuade her. In addition, Moray was beginning to wonder how close the relationship was now between her and Bothwell. Her explanation of why she had gone off so suddenly to Coldinghame that day had been very unconvincing. It was known – although not spoken about – that Bothwell had been there. It was a curious coincidence that she should wish merely to pay the newly married pair a visit at that particular time. If Bothwell were brought back and put in prison, she would find a way of getting him out, and the trouble would start all over again.

Meanwhile, Sir Thomas Dacre had managed to get Bothwell transferred into the keeping of Northumberland's brother, Sir Henry Percy. Bothwell and Sir Henry had met many times along the Borders. There was considerable mutual respect, even friendship. At the Percy stronghold of Tynemouth, Bothwell was more of a guest than a captive, being hospitably treated and receiving visitors whenever he wished. It is not surprising that the next letter to go down to London came from Sir Henry. It was now February 1563. The letter strongly urged Cecil to obtain good terms and consideration for Bothwell. He pointed out that Bothwell's affairs at home were suffering from his being held a prisoner. 'The Earl,' he told the sceptical Cecil, 'is very wise, and not the man he was reported to be.'

The next advice to Cecil came from Moray. It would be far better for all concerned if Bothwell were kept in England as long as possible, preferably in some secure prison. There would only be more trouble between the two countries if he were returned to Scotland. Moray explained the likelihood of Mary's engineering his release if he were returned to a Scottish prison.

It only now remained for Mary's own opinion to be made known. Bothwell was, of course, officially her escaped prisoner. Moray stressed to Cecil that what she might say about it would be of no importance. However, the question was put to her. Her exact reply is not recorded. According to Randolph, who is reported to have been the person charged officially with getting her opinion, she said: 'I take it in good part that my sister's officers, for good will towards me, have apprehended the Lord Bothwell. He hath over-greatly failed towards me. Wherefore I pray you write unto the Queen that I do desire he may be sent hither again unto Scotland.' Randolph reported this at once to Cecil, but added a postscript of his own: 'In no way should the Earl of Bothwell return, but be disposed of as shall be thought good to the Queen of England.'

John Knox, in his comprehensive, but often biased, *History* of the period, reported: 'Our Queen's answer was that he was no rebel. Therefore she requested that he should have liberty to pass where it pleaseth him.'

Randolph was not at all anxious to see Bothwell return to Scotland in any capacity. If anyone was to be disposed of, Randolph himself might well be a candidate if Bothwell were to regain his freedom. In addition to this, Randolph knew that whatever Mary's express desire might be over the matter, Elizabeth would be liable to do the opposite.

This is what now occurred. Elizabeth sent immediate instructions to Sir Henry Percy to bring Bothwell down to London.

They arrived before the end of March. To Bothwell's continued disappointment, he was taken straight to the Tower of London. He was not given any reason, and was prevented from having an audience with Elizabeth. He was not under the strictest conditions, since there are records of many people visiting him. His presence in London was much commented upon.

It seems that Elizabeth was undecided what she should do about him, if anything at all. She hoped to use him in some way, but could not decide what form this should take. Since the Percy family were speaking highly of him, and the French and Spanish Ambassadors also paid him calls, Elizabeth eventually decided he should be released. By the end of May, he was accordingly allowed to leave the Tower. But Elizabeth kept some control on his movements. He was forbidden to leave the country, and could only stay at places officially approved beforehand. Life was again very difficult for him. He had practically no money at all, and no way of getting any. He had no occupation and could do nothing. Without permission to go abroad, he was neutralised. In addition to this, he still could not obtain an audience of the Queen to try for her permission to go to France. It was a sad time for him. Randolph was delighted to mention to Cecil that he was now 'a very beggar, stark naked, naught'.

Bothwell might well have been in considerable straits, but he was far from being 'naught'. The ill-disposed spy was to see him created a duke before the final curtain fell. Whatever his destiny, Bothwell at the moment was in urgent need. News came from the half-forgotten Anna Throndssen. The Register of the Privy Council records the fact that she applied for a passport to travel back to Norway with as many possessions as she wished, during the very time that Bothwell was being detained in the north. From Norway, she sent Bothwell in London something which remains to this day a mystery. It was described at the time as 'a Portugal piece for a token'. No more explanation has come to light. Opinion is divided on what its purpose could have been.

It seems likely that Anna had heard that he was imprisoned. Being a sentimental girl, but having nothing more to give him, she sent him the coin to let him know that he was still in her thoughts. Perhaps her journey to Norway was to see if she could do anything to help him from her own country. She might herself have feared persecution now that Bothwell's own career seemed to be coming to an end. She may have thought it no longer safe to stay in Scotland, although she had a passport granting her protection by the Queen of Scots. There is no mention of the baby boy William; he probably lived with his grandmother at Morham.

Until the outbreak of plague which struck London later that summer, nothing more is heard of Bothwell. But as soon as the disease began to take hold, everyone who had the means went out into the country. The Percy family, being approved guardians of the paroled Bothwell, invited him to come north again until the plague had died away. He was glad to accept such hospitality and shortly arrived at Norham Castle, on the south bank of the Tweed some eight miles from Berwick.

There was probably some unease north of the Border, the Tweed itself, at the return of Bothwell so near to Scotland. But he wished only to travel to France. Until such time as he could do that, he was content to enjoy the company of Sir Henry Percy at Norham. He soon repaid this kindness in a way in which he was well qualified. During Sir Henry's absence from Norham, the authorities at Berwick chose that moment to attempt an enforcement of some unspecified instructions with which Sir Henry had refused to comply. They assailed the small fortress of Norham with the idea of putting matters in order quickly, in the absence of the owner. They may have forgotten whom Sir Henry had left behind.

They were soon reminded. It did not take long for his guest's generalship to assert itself. The eager and unsuspecting force from Berwick was met by a defensive action which scattered them. They returned in disarray to Berwick, reporting their mission uncompleted.

As a result of this reminder that Bothwell might still be dangerous, the English Warden, Sir John Forster, ordered Bothwell's removal from the district down to the Castle of Alnwick. This was the property of Sir Henry's brother, the Earl, but inhabited by the Warden during Northumberland's tour of duty at Court in London. Bothwell was similarly well treated. Here, he turned his energies to horse-coping. Alnwick lay on a useful route for the buying and selling of horses. Bothwell's success at it soon became widely known. Randolph the spy, unable to leave Bothwell alone even when down in London reporting to Cecil, got to hear of it. It would not be long, thought Randolph, before the trade in horses turned to something more sinister. He obtained Cecil's approval to make a closer investigation and, if possible, put a stop to it.

He went to Alnwick itself. His arch enemy received him without the incivilities which Randolph had evidently expected. He was almost surprised at Bothwell's tone. Bothwell could not afford to quarrel with anyone, and even tried to soften Randolph's attitude towards him. But when Bothwell hinted that Randolph might perhaps become a little less obstructive and unfriendly, and even help him to some form of reinstatement in Scotland, the spy began to dissociate himself. It was only when Bothwell mentioned that he was seriously thinking of leaving the country, if only he could get the English Queen's permission, that Randolph softened. He did not look forward to the day when Bothwell might be a free man again in Scotland. Once abroad, he would surely not return. Randolph passed on details of the interview and his general ideas on the 'prisoner' to Cecil. 'Little good he does where he is,' he reported. 'I wish he were out of the country, for neither can he afford it a good word, nor will ever do it a good deed.'

But whatever Randolph's attitude was, it is clear that Bothwell was constantly in touch with Mary. She knew that he could do nothing for her, nor she for him, at this stage. He would indeed be better off in France. Although undocumented, it is almost certain that Mary and Bothwell met again somewhere along the east coast during his stay at Alnwick. It may well have been at Coldinghame, for her favourite half-brother, Lord John Stewart of Coldinghame, had just died while on judicial work for her in Inverness. Mary had been very fond of him and of Bothwell's sister Janet, now left a widow at Coldinghame. It would be natural enough for Mary to go down to console her. Bothwell, too, would have wanted to see his sister at such a sad time. He would have seen his nephew, Francis, then only a few months old. He was to grow up a wild man, too, full worthy of the earldom of Bothwell, which came to him fifteen years later. But it brought him no luck and the title perished with him.

Moray was convinced the Queen had seen Bothwell. Apprehension grew in the Protestant camp at what plans might be hatching. Shortly afterwards, Mary recommended Bothwell for the appointment of Captain of the Scottish Guard at the Court of the King of France, which had become available. This was traditionally at the disposal of the King or Queen of Scotland. It carried prestige and a salary with which Bothwell could pay his mess bills.

But it was of little use if he could not get to France. Mary wrote to Elizabeth, praying her 'dearest sister to give command that the said Earl may have freedom to depart forth at your Realm to such countries as shall seem to him most convenient——.' Bothwell asked as many influential friends as he could find to support his petition to Elizabeth. The Earl of Northumberland, now back from London, readily gave it, as did his brother, Sir Henry. Sir John Forster added his name. Bothwell also wrote, rather surprisingly, to the Earl of Lennox, who lived in Yorkshire, inviting his support. From this it seems that the name of the Lennox's son, Darnley, had already been gaining currency in Mary's affairs. Elizabeth herself was known to approve of Darnley.

A mention from the Earl of Lennox might have been useful in the general petitioning of the Queen. Another surprising source of support was from the odious Randolph. At the end of a fulsome and ambiguous letter, Randolph says to Cecil: '. . . I trouble you with my desire that by your means he [Bothwell] may find favour at the Queen Majesty's hands.' Spoiling the effect of this apparently charitable request, he added that Bothwell was now 'of so little worth that it is no matter where he is'.

Whatever the real motives of the writers of some of his recommendations, Bothwell was in no position to be too selective. His spirits began to rise. Surely Elizabeth would now give him permission to leave the country, once she saw all these letters?

It is not easy to guess what plans Bothwell had in mind as he made preparations to go back to London. It is unlikely he had put out of his head all idea of an eventual return to Scotland. It was obvious to him that he could do nothing there at the moment. But Mary's increasing resentment at the hold her half-brother Moray had over her was no secret. Who could tell how soon there might not be a change in Moray's own fortunes, as dramatic as those of his own? The Earl of Bothwell, confidant of the Queen, Lord High Admiral, Lieutenant of the Borders, had practically overnight become a penniless prisoner in a North Country dungeon. It was true that matters were improving a little now. But if this could happen to the Earl of Bothwell, could it not also happen to the Earl of Moray? And then who would there be to help the young Queen rule?

He raised what last amounts of money his faded credit could still stand. Various friends and men of business paid him visits during the last day of February and the beginning of March. These included David Chalmers, the Edinburgh lawyer who had extricated himself from the Rively affair at Berrington. Bothwell was well informed of all that went on in Scotland.

Later that month of March 1564, he trotted south from Tynemouth. He may have permitted himself a smile as he said goodbye to the Percy family. Fate was known to play _ricks. Why not a trick on the Earl of Moray for a change?

10

THE MOST INTENSIVE search has not brought to light any reliable evidence of where Bothwell spent the next six months. It would be supposed that he went at once to London to get the permission to leave the country, which he wanted so much. But the State papers and Court records do not mention him. It was rumoured that he made repeated applications to see Elizabeth, that each time he was turned away. It was said that Elizabeth was waiting to see how Mary's matrimonial affairs would turn out before she allowed Bothwell to leave England. Knowing that Bothwell enjoyed Mary's confidence to a certain extent, she may have thought that Bothwell, under threat of being returned to the Tower, might be useful if Mary became engaged to someone politically inconvenient to Elizabeth. For the English Queen was constantly worried about Mary's claim to her throne. If she married a Spaniard, or even a Frenchman, the threat to Elizabeth might become very real. It would be far better to produce someone herself and induce Mary to marry him.

Elizabeth had just such a person to suggest for this important office. It was Henry Stewart, better known as Lord Darnley, son of the Earl and Countess of Lennox. Darnley had a tenuous claim himself to succession to the throne of Scotland and England after Elizabeth. It would be very convenient to have Mary married to an English, or rather Scottish, prince of Elizabeth's choosing. This would preclude any foreign attempt on the English throne through Mary or Scotland. It would also mean that there would be no speculation about the succession after Elizabeth's death. Indecision about such matters was very unsettling for a country.

As a monarch's powers began to fail through illness or old age, the jostling for possible succession could be very disruptive. It was also unseemly and did not make for a peaceful close to a reign. Elizabeth considered all these things, although she did not visualise giving up for many a long year. It is also clear that she never intended to marry. If she had ever wished to marry, she would certainly have done so. Any prince would gladly have put up with her biting tongue, mean temper, and repellent personality to enjoy the benefits of the treasury, possessions, and power of England.

Darnley was now pushed forward. Tall, blond, lascivious and athletic, the lad, thought Elizabeth, might well get Mary to marry him. The Scottish Court was frequented mostly by uncouth, middle-aged ruffians, shouting, belching, and fighting, down the corridors of draughty keeps. A slim, dainty youth, very fond of hunting and a great horseman, might prove very attractive to Mary. The parents were agreeable to the enterprise. But it would, his father shrewdly suggested, cost a little more money than he could afford at the moment to see that his son put on a good show. Would her Majesty agree to a subsidy while the courtship was in progress?

Elizabeth was keen enough on the match to authorise a payment of seven hundred pounds for the purpose. The great experiment had started.

It was thought that Darnley had been sent to France, before Mary's return to Scotland, to test her reactions to him even at that early stage. This, if true, may have been a mother's subtle move to fulfil plans she had laid for her favourite son. It may have been evidence of a more long-sighted official scheme set in motion by Elizabeth before Mary had even decided to come back to Scotland.

But whatever the truth of it, Lennox went north with his son. At Wemyss Castle, the great house standing on the cliff above the Forth, Mary waited. Darnley rode up. To him, one woman was much the same as another. But for Mary, he was something special.

The window where she sat is pointed out to this day. With its lawns and brilliant flowers, the house is still the home of the Wemyss family.

It is difficult to imagine Bothwell living throughout the summer in obscurity. He must many times have tried to put his name forward for an audience with Elizabeth. Cecil could have prevented him succeeding. Eventually he took the matter into his own hands in typical fashion. He resorted once more to direct action.

On 12th September the Queen was crossing the open ground at Harrow, surrounded by the usual large throng of courtiers, servants, and soldiers. As she came in leisurely fashion up the rise, a figure on horseback came through the crowd towards her. His clothes were not the finest, noted one of the onlookers, nor was his mount. But there was something commanding about his presence. The air of latent authority with which he sat his horse caused the courtiers to fall back and allow him to pass. He came straight to the Queen herself.

In fluent French, he announced who he was. He pulled out his letters of commendation and mentioned that the Queen of Scots had preferred him to an appointment at the Court of France. He asked the Queen for her permission to leave the country after so long a stay at her command. Cornered in this way, and with no excuse to prevaricate, Elizabeth thought of a way to sidestep the issue neatly. She told Bothwell that he had her commission to carry some papers to the Ambassador in France and could leave at once. In this way, she avoided releasing him from his parole, yet gave him the permission he needed.

Once more Bothwell crossed the Channel to France. By early November he had set up house in Paris, expecting to take over command of the Scottish Guard. But to begin with, nothing came of this. He became a prey to increasing boredom. By all accounts, many of them undoubtedly malicious, but some probably true, his way of life was not as dignified as might be expected from a nobleman awaiting appointment to the royal household.

Bothwell's resurgence in France had been noted in Scotland with displeasure by Moray. Secretary Maitland of Lethington offered to see what could be done to prevent any further progress, perhaps even to bring the matter to an end altogether. He bribed a man called John Wemyss to suborn Bothwell's servants into making an attempt on their master's life. To persuade them into such a course of danger and disloyalty, Wemyss told them of the massive punishments which would fall on their friends and family at home in Scotland, if they refused the attempt or failed in the effort. Urged on by promises of a handsome reward, Bothwell's servants planned to assassinate him. This and the subsequent unlikely story was told by one of the servants much later, when arrested and threatened with torture. The truth must therefore be in question.

But apparently the first attempt was to be by poison, mixed by Bothwell's own barber. To have a barber on his staff indicates that Bothwell was at least attempting to keep up appearances while hovering round the French Court. Although the poison was prepared, no one felt brave enough to offer it to his master. What if it failed to do its work, or the Earl detected its presence before drinking it? Neither groom, barber, page, nor any of the others, cared to contemplate their last few moments trying to explain it away.

The second plan was to be a more manly affair. They would all creep up the stairs together and stab their master as he sat alone in his room one evening. They would be five or six to one, and success would be assured. But the same difficulty arose. Who was to enter the room first? Who to strike the first blow? Five or six to one were not considered reasonable odds when dealing with the Earl of Bothwell, even though he might be surprised alone, unarmed and in a chair with his back to them.

They all felt it was better to leave it for the time being, and risk the wrath of Secretary Maitland at the non-compliance with his orders. They gave up the idea and hoped no more would be said about it. But one of them, a man called Dandie Pringle, did not care to wait for the Earl to start asking awkward questions. He left and took a position with James Murray of Purdovis, yet another minor spy and small-time traitor in the pay of Cecil.

James Murray soon left for Scotland. He carried dispatches to Mary from her uncle, the Cardinal of Lorraine. Bothwell could not have known of James Murray's double dealing, since he asked him to take a note to Mary reminding her of her recommendations about the Scottish Guard. Still nothing had happened about Bothwell taking over the command. James Murray, in fact, called in at Cecil's house on his way back. Together with the disloyal

Dandie Pringle, they made a good source of gossip about Both-well. James Murray reported to Randolph, when he later reached Edinburgh, that Bothwell had asked him to put in a good word with Mary on his behalf about the Scottish Guard.

By chance at this moment, serious indiscipline occurred among the German mercenary troops of the so-called Scottish Guard. Some of them had been following their trade in English regiments before coming to their present posting. They were hard men, with little time for religious devotion or non-military affairs. Daily church parades and the frequent hearing of Mass did not accord with their idea of being mercenaries. They soon became out of hand. It was so essential to have loyal and well-disciplined troops so close to the sovereign and the heart of the government, that Bothwell's appointment was at last confirmed. Throckmorton, Elizabeth's Ambassador, reported the news to Cecil on 10th February.

At last it seemed that the turbulent Earl of Bothwell had found a useful occupation in a position of importance and prestige, well paid and entirely suited to his ability and inclination.

'But,' says Bothwell in his own memoirs, 'no sooner had I received these benefits than I received a command by letter from the Queen of Scots to return to Scotland——.'

A little over three weeks after taking up his appointment, Bothwell appeared in Edinburgh.

Astonishment was widespread. Whatever would the Earl of Bothwell do now? The Earl of Moray was beside himself with rage and stormed into Mary's presence. The Queen did not mention having written to Bothwell. It cannot be certain that she did get in touch with him at all on this occasion. It is unlikely she summoned him home. For she had just met Henry Stewart, Lord Darnley, at Wemyss. She was much intrigued and thought she would like to know him better. Bothwell she knew already. He would come to her whenever she sent the word.

Moray insisted on some action being taken about Bothwell. The Queen must sanction his proclamation as an outlaw, an escaped prisoner, he must be 'put to the horn', a public and official denunciation.

Mary was too taken up with the possibilities of Darnley to go into it any further. To stimulate her into greater activity over the return of the great enemy, Moray arranged for James Murray of Purdovis and Dandie Pringle, Bothwell's former servant, to come before Mary and retail all manner of gossip about Bothwell in Paris. With no one to corroborate or deny what they said, Mary gradually became incensed as one story after another was told with increasing detail. All the names they said he had called her, all the things they said he threatened to do to her when he got back – the stories became more and more colourful. Randolph, of course, was present, adding what titbits he could think of on the spur of the moment. Cecil was delighted with his report of the whole affair. For Mary, out of exasperation, or belief of the stories, or possibly just to bring their cacophonous shouting of gossip to an end and relieve her headache, agreed to have Bothwell summoned to answer charges.

Trial was fixed for 2nd May in Edinburgh. Bothwell had not been present nor been called to appear before Mary. Moray had seen to that. He was determined this time to eliminate Bothwell for all time. Bothwell knew he was in personal danger from Moray, who hoped to lay hands on him before the trial, on the pretext that he had been found escaping before answering the charges. But Bothwell did not intend to fall into Moray's clutches at this stage. He knew he would never get himself out. He paid in two hundred pounds as evidence of his acceptance of the trial, and of his intention to appear and defend himself. He then went down to his great fortress of the Hermitage. One of the Elliots, traditional opponents of the Hepburns, had got hold of it while Bothwell was away. But he was soon turned out. Bothwell gathered round him many of his Borderers, who were prepared to stay loyal to him whatever he had done and whatever the cost to themselves.

But it was rumoured throughout the Borders that Moray did not intend to wait even now for the date of the trial. A message came to the Hermitage that Moray meant to surround the huge castle at night. Bothwell had no intention of being trapped in bed a second time. He went out during the darkness with a large company of horsemen on to the low hills round the Hermitage. It would not have gone well with the Earl of Moray if he had indeed had the temerity to pursue the Borderer into his lair.

Bothwell returned at dawn. But during the day he realised that the time was not yet ripe for him to have returned to Scotland. He went through to Crichton, and then back to his mother at Morham. From there he made his way to North Berwick and once more took ship to France.

Back in Edinburgh, the law took its course. But Moray did not feel justice could be left to steer true. He raised an army of over five thousand men. They clanked into Edinburgh the day before the trial was due and occupied the centre of the city. With him and his multitude of friends and supporters was the Lord Chief Justice, who was to conduct the trial and pronounce sentence. This was the Earl of Argyle, Moray's brother-in-law. Seeing the size of Moray's army, Argyle declared himself strongly in favour of Moray's cause. His support was usually given to whoever at the time seemed to have the advantage. On this occasion, it was certainly the Earl of Moray.

This travesty of a trial was held despite the absence of the accused. In his defence, Bothwell's cousin, a Hepburn of Riccarton, bravely spoke up for him. He pointed out the unlikelihood of Bothwell getting a fair trial under these loaded conditions. So effective was his defence, that Moray was merely made to look ridiculous. Mary let it be known that she would not consent to any verdict other than forfeiture of the two hundred pounds. The whole case then collapsed and Moray withdrew extremely angry.

There was more to make him angry. Mary and Darnley had certainly fallen briefly in love as a result of an attack of measles suffered by Darnley. Mary herself had nursed him tenderly and devotedly. As has happened many a time with nurse and patient, they decided to marry as soon as the patient recovered.

For Moray, this looked like being a disaster to his own prospects. There would now be a Catholic King, who would certainly usurp Moray's position. They would almost certainly have children, which would ensure the line of succession to the Scottish throne, and also to the English throne. Catholicism would return to Scotland, and there would be no place for the leader of a Protestant faction against the religious tyranny of a Catholic Queen.

Elizabeth also awoke to the danger and inconvenience of the impending marriage which she had been instrumental in bringing about. What could she have been thinking of, allowing the match so nearly to be completed? It was intended merely to delay and deflect Mary from any more serious entanglement abroad. Lennox must return at once to England and bring Darnley back with him.

But neither father nor son paid any attention. The marriage plan went forward. Elizabeth danced with rage and imprisoned Darnley's mother, who had stayed behind.

It was no use. In consultation with Cecil, Randolph suggested kidnapping Darnley and Mary under some pretext, even murdering them. Several plans to snatch the couple away and bring them to an English prison were hurriedly worked out. One was even half-heartedly tried near Perth by Lord Rothes, but it came to nothing.

Mary and Darnley were privately and secretly married on 9th July, leaving a State occasion until later. The news was brought to Bothwell back in his Paris lodgings. He had not recovered the Captaincy of the Scottish Guard. Once more he was in France with nothing to do and resources dwindling rapidly in the gaiety of Paris life. Although Moray's influence might now be on the wane with a new and Catholic King for Mary, none of it was much help to the exiled Bothwell. Would Mary have any need of him now? What was he to do?

In the excitement of getting ready for her State wedding on 29th July, and busy with new clothes for herself and her husband, Mary paid no attention at all to the disgruntled, and therefore highly dangerous, Earl of Moray. The couple careered about the country holding dances, banquets, tournaments, and hunting expeditions. On 16th July, seeing Darnley did not appear to be showing many qualities needed for a general or chief of staff, Mary thought she would be safer if Bothwell took charge of all these matters. Moray, she saw, could not really be relied upon any longer. He seemed very petulant and cross these days, she noted. Never mind. James Bothwell was the one to put it all straight. She signed a summons to him to stop doing whatever he was doing and come back at once. All was forgiven. He was to make up an army, or whatever he thought necessary, and defend everything properly from all the sour-faced people who kept clumping round in armour. Signing the letter with a gay flourish, she whirled back into the more serious business of planning the music, doing the flowers, and inviting the guests.

Bothwell, wandering uneasily on the fringe of the constant revelries at the French Court, never received that summons. The Queen had thrust it into the hand of that same Hepburn of Riccarton who had stood up in Bothwell's defence at the Edinburgh trial. This was all observed by Randolph. Cecil warned his agents and the various Wardens to watch for Bothwell at all costs and not let him through. Riccarton himself was seized over the Border by the Earl of Bedford, who communicated Mary's letter at once to Cecil.

Mary went through her magnificent wedding on the Sunday of 29th July, unaware that her loyal would-be defender was kicking his heels in Paris, waiting vainly for the call.

As time went by and Bothwell neither arrived nor sent word, Mary became alarmed. She began to see already that Darnley was hopeless. The fires of love had died almost before the wedding, certainly soon afterwards. The statesmanship and leadership she had hoped for from her husband did not exist. Wherever was Bothwell? Panic began to rise in the young Queen.

She sent another messenger. Bothwell must come at once. This time the summons got through to the despondent Bothwell.

His spirits soared. He left Paris the same day, moving with such suddenness that Cecil's specially deputed spies lost the trail. Bothwell's instructions this time took him to Brussels. At Aershott, nearby, he had a meeting with the Duchess of Aershott, who was a cousin of Mary's, and William Yaxley, Darnley's English Secretary. Good staff work had gone into the arrangement of this conference at such short notice. The agenda does not survive. But evidently Mary and Darnley had been making tentative inquiries about what help they might be able to rely on from the Continent, if the situation deteriorated any more.

By this time Bothwell had been found by Cecil's men. Elaborate arrangements were made to trap or intercept him as he made his way back to Scotland. English warships patrolled the northern, western, and Irish approaches. HMS *Aid,* a famous two-hundred-and-fifty-ton vessel, fast, and heavily armed, under the command of the well-known explorer, Captain Anthony Jenkinson, was given the duty of watching the eastern approaches, particularly the Firth of Forth. Elizabeth and Cecil realised that their chances of bolstering up the Earl of Moray again and restoring him to his position in Scotland would be greatly reduced, if Mary once more had Bothwell to rely upon.

But Bothwell was equal to the occasion. Not travelling in a borrowed warship, which Cecil's men had expected, he took charge of a small, very fast vessel of shallow draught. Cutting across the narrow reach of the North Sea, he sailed at speed up the coast, hugging the inshore waters. By 17th September 1565, he had reached the mouth of the river Tweed. Here the whole journey nearly came to a disastrous end. In the hopes of currying favour with Elizabeth's naval authorities, two privateers, or private pirate vessels, the property of Captain Charles Wilson, had offered to help in the interception of Bothwell, or of anyone who might be working for Mary against Elizabeth. The licensed brigands were lying in wait right in the river mouth. Coastal fog covered the estuary thickly as Bothwell's little ship drifted in on the tide. Soon the mist lifted over the still water. Bothwell's ship and Captain Wilson's pirates lay almost alongside each other. Bothwell reacted the quickest, everyone rushed to the oars and rowed for the open sea. Captain Wilson opened fire with all his guns, but Bothwell was below the level to which the Captain could depress his guns. As the elevation improved, the rowers got quickly out of range, caught the offshore breeze and were gone. But it had been a near thing.

Later that same day, Bothwell put into the fishing harbour at Eyemouth. Within fifteen minutes of making fast, Bothwell had collected horses, unloaded the quantity of guns, powder, shot, and other equipment he had brought from Brussels at Yaxley's arrangement, and was heading inland for Edinburgh and the Queen.

Meanwhile, events had taken a serious turn. Barely a month after the happy wedding, the country had been divided once more into the old Protestant and Catholic divisions. Moray, leader of the Protestants, had come out in open revolt against his half-sister and her husband. Galled by the eclipse of his power over Mary and the nation's affairs, Moray had been made even more venomous by insults from Darnley. The young King had even suggested that Moray owned far too much land: he might care to give some of it up? Moray did not like this approach. It earned Darnley a good measure of hatred and enmity.

It was not difficult after this to persuade all the Protestants, with the old Duke of Châtelherault and all the Hamiltons, that their days were numbered unless they did something to check the growing Catholic influence at Court.

In opposition, led ineffectually by Darnley, but enthusiastically by Mary, were the Catholic royalists. Darnley's father, Lennox, the Earl of Atholl, and Lord George Gordon, now Earl of Huntly, were the Catholic leaders. They had more men than Moray, but had no capable general.

But there was no real battlefield. When Moray advanced on Edinburgh on 30th August, with many less troops, the royalists retreated to Stirling and Glasgow. Most people were not quite sure what any fight would really be about. Moray was the only one with a clear objective: to get rid of Darnley, perhaps Mary as well, establish himself as regent, ruler or king, and prevent Bothwell having anything to do with it.

Moray accordingly found himself in possession of Edinburgh, but not of the castle. Lord Erskine, the Keeper, threatened to blow up everything and everyone in range of his guns if either side attacked him. It was not clear from this whose side he was on.

It was now rather an anti-climax for Moray. No one gave battle. There seemed nowhere to go and nothing to do. His army was very expensive to maintain. Two days later, at three o'clock in the morning, he had the withdrawal sounded. The Protestant force went off westwards. Mary now left her army at Stirling and came back to Holyrood. Darnley had lost interest in military affairs and had gone hunting and hawking.

On 21st September, Bothwell arrived from Eyemouth in company with David Chalmers, his faithful Edinburgh lawyer friend. With him he brought his small train of men and munitions.

Mary received him delightedly, according to the reports. He told her all his news, and passed on the promises of troops and armaments she might call on from France, if need arose.

Darnley evidently welcomed Bothwell with relief and goodwill. He was probably glad to have someone reliable to take charge of affairs, and presumably without pretensions to usurp his kingly position.

Mary at once created Bothwell Lieutenant of the Borders again. He appointed himself Chief of Staff as well, and drew up detailed plans for ridding Scotland of the Queen's enemies. The first step would be the reforming and augmenting of the army she had left at Stirling. By the end of the month, he calculated they could move out of Stirling fifteen thousand strong and sweep the rebels over the Border and into the sea. If they stood their ground, he assured her, her army would annihilate the enemy.

Mary, of course, hoped there would be no actual fighting. Perhaps by the end of the month the rebels would all have gone home, having seen who was now to command her troops.

After making all the arrangements, Bothwell went down to the Borders for a few days to reassert his authority and to let everyone know he was firmly back in the saddle, bearing the Queen's commission. Once more one of his permanent adversaries had got hold of the Hermitage castle during his absence. This time it was a Robert Elliot. The impudent intruder lasted no longer than others who had tried the same thing, when Bothwell had been in prison or temporary exile.

After his first enthusiasm at meeting Bothwell had died away, Darnley began to think the returning Lieutenant had become a little too important rather too quickly.

He, Darnley, was the King of Scotland – if only more people would realise it – and the Queen's army should surely be commanded by the King. What was more, it was now confirmed that the rebels had converged on Dumfries, near the western end of the Scottish border: Darnley's father, the Earl of Lennox, had been made Lieutenant of the Western Border, which included this very district. It was, said Darnley to Mary, perfectly clear that the actual commander of any operations in that district should therefore be the Warden of the Western Marches and father of the King, the Earl of Lennox.

Mary laughed. Neither father nor son knew anything about soldiers and campaigns, she told Darnley. Far better leave it to Bothwell, who really knew how the thing should be managed. And she suggested a dark bay horse with a white blaze to its forehead would show off Darnley's new armour admirably. But Darnley was in no mood for jokes. It was his first row with his wife. Had Mary already begun to mock him? Was her love and respect beginning to ebb after such a short time?

There are signs that this was the case. Darnley was furious. Mary would have been wiser to suggest a compromise, which could have left the King in theoretical command, with his father a field commander, and Bothwell to do all the work a little further behind the scenes.

The wrangling went on for a week. Mary could be as adamant as the petulant Darnley. Bothwell finally told her that if she did not settle the row, the enemy would have vanished altogether, intact and unscathed, ready to strike another day. Mary gave in. Darnley should be Commander-in-Chief, provided he gave no orders, and his father, Lennox, should lead the troops on the western sector.

But, by the time the army had got on the move, it was, as Bothwell had predicted, far too late to catch the rebels. Darnley spent the time trying on different sorts of armour, when he should have been reviewing troops and discussing plans with the others. Mary gave great encouragement by galloping about on a white horse with a blue and crimson cloak billowing round her damascened breastplate. On her head a tiny helmet of burnished steel, with a long white feather, made unsuccessful efforts to contain her cascade of chestnut hair. On her saddle-bow were two huge pistols. She needed two hands to hold one up, and could never have fired it. At her side, she wore a rapier, its blade mirror-bright as she flourished it out of its gem-studded scabbard. The effect was superlative. The troops adored her. The whole army surged forward in the greatest of spirits.

But by the time they got to the Border, Moray was practically in Carlisle. Urgent messages had brought English troops under the Earl of Bedford rushing to save him from the royal vengeance.

The forces never met. For Moray, it was a disaster, without even an honourable defeat in battle. For Mary, it was a triumph. She had led a victorious army through her realm without a shot having to be fired.

For Bothwell the success was particularly sweet. He had planned the Queen's campaign for her and in practice commanded her army. And Moray, the old enemy, had been driven over the Border into England. For a man who had lain penniless in an

English gaol a few months before, and only a few weeks earlier had wandered practically a vagrant throught the streets of London, it was not a bad recovery.

11

SINCE THERE WAS no standing army, and no apparent enemy in the country to warrant the cost of maintaining one, the majority of Mary's force was disbanded at once. Mary and Darnley went back to Edinburgh to resume the normal activities of the Court.

Bothwell stayed behind at Dumfries with some fifteen hundred men to make sure the rebels did not think of coming back again. Mary was particularly gratified at being able to leave the situation in his hands. When he returned to Edinburgh at the end of October, Mary asked him to undertake a general reorganisation and refurbishing of all the defences of the country. At that time, the only country which really mattered was from the Border in the south, to a line running roughly westwards from Dundee. North of this, the population was so scattered that an occasional judicial progress was quite adequate to maintain order and to see that no danger threatened the capital. Bothwell undertook this with great vigour. All the major defences were overhauled, and the methods of raising men and arms were thoroughly reviewed.

No more was heard from Moray for the time being. His defeat had also been a defeat for Elizabeth, Cecil and all the English party. It was particularly annoying for Cecil, since nearly all his spies, informers and quislings had been swept away with Moray, or had felt it advisable to stay in England for the time being. As a result Cecil's information from Scotland began to dry up. There was also no useful person who could distribute the customary bribes to keep Scottish loyalty to the Crown at a minimum.

Elizabeth therefore proposed that there should be a new joint Conference to discuss the peaceful conduct of affairs on both sides along the Border. Bothwell's vigorous establishment of discipline since his return had provoked some dissatisfaction along the English side. During the winter, when nothing could be done in the way of farming, it was customary to make regular raids back and forth across the Border, both as an occupation and in order to keep stocks of fodder and livestock from getting too low.

These raids sometimes got out of hand, so that troops had to intervene. On the English side, there were regular garrisons available on call, either to restrain or protect their own people. On the Scottish side, matters were left entirely to the Borderers, since there were no regular troops. Permanent arrangements to keep the peace would benefit both sides. Mary agreed to the Conference. But Elizabeth was interested in the Conference for reasons in addition to her proper concern for the welfare of her outlying communities. Regular meetings with delegates from Scotland would fill the gap in her lines of information in Scotland, now that the rebels were all in exile. It was necessary, of course, for the Scottish delegates to be thoroughly disloyal and prepared to give away all they knew about the confidential affairs of their country. Such delegates, unfortunately, were never rare. Randolph, the agent of Cecil and Elizabeth, was to see that the Scottish delegates came into this category. He did not anticipate any difficulty in suggesting suitable names to Mary.

But Mary appointed Bothwell.

Randolph was aghast, Cecil and Elizabeth furious. The Conference could now serve no useful purpose. At least, not for Elizabeth.

Bothwell himself was indifferent to their opinions. He was more concerned with the opinion of Lady Jean Gordon, the twenty-year-old sister of the new Earl of Huntly, and a great favourite of Queen Mary's. Encouraged by the Queen on many occasions, Bothwell proposed to Lady Jean. There is much evidence of Mary's encouragement of Lady Jean to accept the hand of her Lieutenant, which she did.

Lady Jean was another girl with a good business head, like the Anna Throndssen of whom nothing is heard at the moment. Anna was either abroad among her family, or back in Scotland living unobtrusively in the unknown dwelling given to her by Bothwell. Lady Jean later married the Earl of Sutherland. From the family papers, still in the great Sutherland castle of Dunrobin, Lady Jean can be seen to have been a most formidable woman, at least in her later years, personally managing and developing her husband's huge estates. On the Earl of Sutherland's death, she married yet again. The Alexander Ogilvie she finally married was the man she would have liked to have married to begin with. They were sweethearts. But Ogilvie became engaged to another girl. Within weeks Lady Jean had married Bothwell. It may only have been because of Queen Mary's persistent suggestions, in order to cheer her up and give a new reason for living, that Lady Jean married Bothwell.

There is no evidence of any great love between them. The wedding went off well enough in spite of certain difficulties about where it should be held. Mary was most anxious that it should be held during a Mass at the royal chapel at Holyrood. Lady Jean, from the strong Catholic family of the Gordons of Huntly, was quite agreeable. But Bothwell, who had, as far as is known, never attended a Mass, was not going to start on his wedding day. The church in the Canongate, the old street of Edinburgh, was finally agreed upon. Mary gave Lady Jean all the material for her wedding dress. As recorded in the palace inventory, this was twelve yards of cloth of silver, and six yards of white taffeta for the train, with anything over to line the sleeves. After the service, conducted by Lady Jean's uncle, the Bishop of Galloway, a wedding breakfast was given for them at Kinloch House nearby.

For the next five days, there were great festivities and tournaments. At most of those Mary was present. Darnley was not always there, but did attend a banquet which Mary and he gave jointly for the bridal couple.

There is much speculation about the legality of the wedding. A document exists at Dunrobin Castle, suggesting that Bothwell, despite being a Protestant, obtained a Papal dispensation beforehand for permission to marry because of the consanguinity, or too-close relationship, of the couple. This dispensation requires the marriage to be *in occulo ecclesiae*, which means, in this case in a Catholic church by Catholic rites. The Bishop of Galloway certainly married them, but not in a Catholic church, and he never went into the pulpit, which would have been customary. This yellowed document has lain for four hundred years in the massive charter room on the cliffs of the North Sea. It has frequently been declared a forgery. It will probably never be known whether the wedding was strictly legal.

It is of academic interest. Even the honeymoon was a disaster. The first week was spent at Seton House, the home of Bothwell's friend, Lord Seton, some ten miles along the coast east of Edinburgh. Towards the end of the week it was reported that they were barely on speaking terms. At the beginning of the next week, Bothwell was back in Edinburgh, by himself. But before he left, he had occasion to meet once more that personification of cunning and malice, Randolph the spy. The tables had been turned on Cecil's most useful agent at last. He had been tricked by a double agent, who told Mary herself that Randolph had handed over large sums of money to him from Elizabeth, to pass on to Moray and the rebels.

Mary insisted on his immediate expulsion. On 2nd March, Randolph had no option but to accompany the Queen's messenger out of Edinburgh, and over the Border. But as he passed Seton Castle, Bothwell came riding out to meet him, Randolph having been told that Bothwell would like a word with him. The spy must have felt apprehensive at meeting his long-time adversary on such equal grounds. But Bothwell intended him no violence. He merely wanted to know why Elizabeth and Cecil had made such strenuous objections to his being appointed Scottish delegate to the proposed Border Conference.

Very wisely, Randolph refused to say anything about this. He merely managed to hint that information obtained from Bothwell's defecting servant, Dandie Pringle, about Bothwell's alleged comments on Queen Elizabeth and various other reported scandals, made him entirely unacceptable to Her Majesty.

Bothwell swore that all the stories were untrue and that he would challenge to combat anyone who repeated them. Randolph would kindly report this to the English Queen. The spy promised to do so. And now a question from Randolph to Bothwell: why was he being so unfairly sent out of Scotland?. According to Randolph's dispatch to Elizabeth, Bothwell replied: 'It is the Queen's will, procured by others than myself.' This was no surprise to Randolph. 'That I know to be true,' he told Bothwell.

They parted, peacefully if not amicably, Randolph with evident relief.

Lady Jean had brought with her a dowry of twelve thousand marks. Bothwell made over to her the whole of the Crichton property. She spent eleven thousand marks of her dowry on redeeming the property from the creditors who had got hold of it. She retained the property until the end of her days, improving and even enlarging the holding.

They had no children. In view of her offspring by her later marriages, it is natural to speculate that something may have been lacking on Bothwell's part. He had not, on other occasions, stinted himself of opportunity to produce children. Later, many more opportunities occurred. The mystery of why he left no recorded offspring through his life remains unsolved.

Bothwell had a miniature painted of Lady Jean at the time of the wedding. If the likeness was a good one, she was not unattractive, despite the unfortunate shape of her nose. But her expression appears unrelenting. No touch of humour creases her bland face. Alexander Ogilvie's engagement was perhaps the chief reason for her marriage to Bothwell. She brought Bothwell neither love nor luck. There is no evidence that she ever tried very hard.

Another newly-married couple with whom things were not going well was Mary and Darnley. Hopelessly inflated by the importance of his position as King Consort, the weakness of Darnley's character found no restraint. His drinking habits went well beyond the bounds of regal hospitality. He was plied with drink by the lascivious and unscrupulous gang which clustered round him. His sporting companions were the most disreputable crew. No woman was safe within his reach. Many were pushed, many needed no pushing. Several claimed they were pregnant by the King, including one of Mary's own household.

Mary herself was now known to be with child. Many attempts have been made to show that Darnley was not responsible for this. But no reliable evidence can be found to support such gossip.

Among the various candidates for fatherhood of her child has been her private secretary in charge of foreign affairs. This was David Rizzio, son of a rich family from Piedmont, and thought by some to have been an agent of the Pope infiltrated into Mary's Court. Mary thought highly of him, but she was in a minority. Rizzio was a fine musician and a good singer. He also had a good brain, and managed nearly all Mary's correspondence with France and Italy. He wrote fluent French and Italian. He was an astute judge of character. It was this which created so much enmity between himself and Mary's other advisers. People became jealous of Rizzio. Chief among these was Darnley. Mary always took Rizzio's advice in preference to any offered by Darnley. It was thought by many of the ineffectual nobles that Rizzio had too much influence over Mary. He was, as was natural for a private secretary, often in her private apartments. Stories of her being found in compromising situations with Rizzio less than fully clothed, can for lack of evidence, be dismissed as malicious lies.

Bothwell was perfectly friendly with Rizzio. Possibly to help Bothwell, Rizzio had been largely responsible for the expulsion of Randolph the spy. Randolph knew this. He had got word of a plot to murder the Italian several days before it was carried out, and wrote all the details to Cecil. He also hinted at a plot to murder Mary.

By March 1566, the undercurrent of plotting and intrigue involving many people and factions had begun to stir the surface. Darnley had never been more than King Consort. This meant that if Mary died, the crown would not pass to her husband. Rizzio was instrumental in persuading Mary not to grant Darnley the 'crown matrimonial'. This would have given the crown to Darnley in the event of Mary's death. Darnley, urged on by unscrupulous friends, was determined to get this new status. It was pointed out to him that only Rizzio stood in his way. If Rizzio were to be removed, and Mary were perhaps not to survive long with her unborn child, why then, the crown would pass to Darnley, whose mother was a Douglas. Many members of the Douglas family thought this an admirable plan. Chief among them was the Earl of Morton, head of the Douglas family. What pickings there would be with a *louche*, malleable young Darnley on the throne! All the opponents of Mary, now in exile in England, could return to Scotland. Everyone would be pleased.

Darnley thought no further than his vision of kingship. Secretly he met Morton and several other rebel leaders and exiles.

He agreed that Rizzio should be murdered, preferably in front of the Queen herself, or at least in her apartment. Darnley's vicious nature asserted itself. Mary would probably not survive such a shock, being well on with her child. After Rizzio's death, all the nobles would insist on the 'crown matrimonial' being granted to Darnley. He would then instruct Mary to pardon all concerned.

Darnley denied that he signed such an agreement. But unfortunately, the document still survives, and can be seen to be no forgery.

There was little secrecy about the plan, yet Mary got no word of it. More surprisingly, neither did Bothwell, Huntly, nor any of the loyal nobles of the Queen.

At eight o'clock on the evening of 9th March, the gaunt and horrible Lord Ruthven rose from his bed of sickness and disease, on which he died a few weeks later. A black breastplate over his nightshirt, he burst in on the Queen, while she was at supper. Other conspirators crowded behind. Rizzio was stabbed to death. Darnley held Mary down. The scene has been described countless times. In his back, as he was flung down the stairs, Mary saw the jewelled stiletto she had been given by her first and dearest husband, Francis II of France, and which she had given as a present to Darnley.

In the guard-commander's quarters, along a passage which had been newly walled up – the conspirators had been thorough – Bothwell, Huntly and Atholl were passing the evening together. The turmoil and tramp of feet sent them running to the only connecting door. It was barred. The sound of a score of voices, the scraping of weapons, rang through the building.

Atholl thought all was up with them and went off to make friends with whomever had created the uproar. But Bothwell's only thought, now he knew what had happened, was to rescue the Queen from the ruffians who had overwhelmed her. With his brother-in-law, Huntly, he squeezed through a small window on the north side, which gave on to a form of dry moat where a few lions were traditionally kept. The lions must have been newly fed, for the two men ran to safety across the enclosure and out into the city.

In Holyrood, the criminals were making their peace with the

Queen. The Lord Provost and citizens of Edinburgh had been assured by Darnley that he and the Queen were well and that there was no cause for alarm. Mary, deeply distressed, yet stimulated into cool action and given physical strength by the horror of the murder, made plans to escape from the close detention in which she was being held. Darnley persuaded her to grant pardons on the spot to most of the conspirators. With an effort, which Mary herself described later, she spoke to Darnley. She took him aside, reasoned with him, subtly pointed out the danger in which he had landed himself at the hands of such ruthless friends.

Two days later, she had wormed the whole story out of him. Very composed, she received Morton and all the others. Like vultures, they had clustered round, offering their loyalty and good service. It was agreed on all sides that Darnley was now to be granted his 'crown matrimonial'. A new Parliament was summoned. In answer to a summons, reputedly from Mary, Moray reappeared from his exile, and assured her he had played no part in the affair. He was now entirely at her loyal service. He took the opportunity of obtaining a pardon for his recent rebellion. Mary was in no position to deny anything. She realised her own life might now be in danger.

But she was not alone. Bothwell had got a message through the heavy guard to her. She persuaded Darnley to get the guard taken off by Monday. The murder had taken place on Saturday. She had also won Darnley round entirely. He was convinced that his former friends would now murder him in due course. Gripped by fear, he implored Mary to save him from them. Steeling herself to touch him, she suffered his embrace. She promised that if he obeyed her exactly, she would save him.

At midnight, with a servant each, they crept down to a side door. The Captain of the Guard and the Master of the Horse were waiting with the best horses Bothwell could produce. In a moment the party was racing for the open country, eastwards along the coast. Darnley trembled so much with fear that he could hardly sit his horse. Riding pillion behind him, his aide-de-camp, Anthony Standen, held him on. Sweat coursed down the quaking limbs of the cowardly King.

Mary, six months pregnant, openly threatened with murder, her clothes still bearing the blood of her faithful secretary and friend, rode proudly, upright and alone on a huge, dark horse specially chosen for her.

Near Seton, her Lieutenant of the Borders, James, Earl of Bothwell, spurred forward out of the gloom to join her. With him were Huntly, Seton, and a few others. They made for the safety of Dunbar, fifteen miles further on. During the night, Mary's horse cast a shoe. They stopped at a village smithy. Bothwell turned the old blacksmith out of his bed. They all gathered round as he blew up his fire and replaced the shoe. The spot is remembered to this day, the place where the Queen stopped to have her horse shod.

At dawn they cantered up to the gaunt castle on the sea. It was hardly furnished at all. Mary was lifted off her great horse. But she was not finished yet. As soon as a fire was lit, she took a pan of eggs and made an omelette for them all. Then, with a joke about what she had learnt in the royal kitchens of France, she lay down to rest.

But for Bothwell, there was no time for rest. The main objective was to get Mary back to Edinburgh with a sizeable force, and re-establish her authority.

In response to Bothwell's call, over four thousand men from the Borders had gathered at Dunbar within three days, pledged to restore the Queen and rout her rebels. It was an amazing feat to have raised so many men so quickly. Their numbers, and the alacrity with which they had assembled, dismayed Morton and all his fellow conspirators. Some started to come forward cautiously to Dunbar seeking a pardon for their part in the plot, or making excuses about why they had not come to her help.

In her usual manner, Mary gave pardons to nearly all of them, except Morton. He had not quite had the audacity to go that far. By the end of the week, Bothwell decided they were ready to move forward. The march began. At Haddington she received a message from her deceitful half-brother, Moray, who again sought pardon, and promised he now had nothing to do with Morton, or anyone who could have behaved so treacherously towards her.

The remainder of the rebels and conspirators faded away over the Border to England. The Earl of Bedford wrote to Cecil saying that Moray had asked him to do all he could for the fugitives, including Morton. So much for Moray's new profession of loyalty to his Queen.

Mary now made a triumphal return to Edinburgh, with Bothwell at the head of her troops. The next few days were spent in rounding up those who had declared themselves for Morton or had been implicated in some way.

Darnley, despised and abhorred by Mary, and ignored by most other people, withdrew deeper into his private life of sport and dissipation. He had many enemies now. Most sinister were all his former accomplices in the Rizzio plot. He had betrayed and doublecrossed them. They knew this well enough. He was a marked man from now on.

Closest to the Queen, and her chief support in everything to do with running the country, was James Hepburn, Earl of Bothwell. 'The Earl of Bothwell,' it was learnt, 'hath now of all men greatest access and familiarity with the Queen, so that nothing of importance is done without him.'

12

FROM THE REGISTER of the Privy Council at the time, the extent of Bothwell's influence in useful legislation can easily be seen. New laws about counterfeit money, inshore poaching by foreign fishing vessels, limitation of pardons for serious offences, and many others, began to appear.

Darnley was absent most of the time. Mary had no wish to have him with her. Her baby was due in a couple of months: she was thankful to be able to leave so many affairs in Bothwell's now patently capable hands.

The Earl of Moray was also absent to begin with. But he was not prepared to stay in obscurity and semi-disgrace, although officially pardoned, while Bothwell ruled the roost. He brazenly appeared at Court after a few weeks, and obtained permission to remain there.

It was clear that there would be trouble between him and Bothwell. Moray meant to get rid of him again, although he realised it might not be as easy as last time. The first manœuvre was one of apparent friendship. Mary invited everyone to a dinner party. Out of deference to her, they all sat down together. Mary was pleased at the apparent success of her efforts at conciliation. She had tried this before, with the same effect and same results.

Bothwell was inclined to try a little intrigue himself in order to discredit his enemy. Darnley was more frightened of Moray than of anyone else. Bothwell therefore joined with Darnley in trying to show how Moray was as much, if not more, to blame for all the rebellion and the murder of Rizzio. Typically, Mary refused to listen to any accusations. Her half-brother, she declared, was now most kindly disposed towards her. Whatever mistakes he had made in the past, he was now sorry for them, and she had completely forgiven him. He would certainly not try anything new to upset her, she was sure. Her chief preoccupation was now the impending birth of her baby. She could not concern herself with past quarrels nor discuss hypothetical future ones. She was sure everyone would now be friends, and would await the arrival of the baby as eagerly as she herself. The formula was her usual one. And as on previous occasions, it was equally faulty.

Moray saw his chance in her increasing inactivity as the time drew near. His main target was the disruption and removal of Bothwell.

He therefore started to foment trouble throughout the Borders with all the people who might be persuaded to go against Bothwell. To support this insidious campaign of persuasion, he had the wholehearted assistance of these rebels who had remained unpardoned in England after his own rebellion, and now after the Rizzio affair. Chief among these was the Earl of Morton himself. In addition to the plan for general subversion, Moray had a plot to do away with Bothwell personally. No details of it have yet come to light. But in August of that year, 1566, the Earl of Bedford, from Berwick, wrote to Cecil: 'I have heard that there is a device working for the Earl of Bothwell, about which I could indeed obtain precise information. But since such things are not addressed to me, I do not wish to hear any more of them. He hath grown of late so hated that he cannot long continue.'

The only way to check the spread of Moray's influence along the Border was to go down under royal command and conduct one of the periodical judicial progresses. Bothwell made plans for this. He issued proclamations giving details of dates and places of assizes along the Border country, and summonses to all the usual people to attend. This would undoubtedly have had the effect of countering any falling off in Bothwell's influence. It would also have checked the spread of lawlessness stimulated by the Queen's rebels over the Border.

Unfortunately for Bothwell, the whole programme had to be cancelled. Mary's baby was about to be born in Edinburgh Castle. Mary drew up a will. Among many bequests of jewellery, she left Bothwell a table-cut diamond set in black enamel, and a tiny figure of a mermaid set in diamonds, holding a diamond mirror and a ruby comb.

On the morning of 19th June 1566, the baby duly arrived after much travail. Like so much connected with Mary, even the birth could not be straightforward. The baby was reported to have been stillborn. Eye-witnesses swore to seeing a baby being hauled up the wall in a basket to the tiny window of her bedroom. The family of the Earl of Mar claim the baby was theirs. Whatever the facts, the baby was hideous, misshapen, huge-tongued, unable to walk until seven years old.

The Earl of Moray had been staying in the castle with her, and also the Earl of Argyle. Bothwell and Huntly wanted to move in as well. But Moray prevented this, Mary being too ill to remonstrate or do anything about it. Moray was beginning to regain his lost control over Mary.

Some five weeks later, Mary went by boat to Alloa, where lived the Earl of Mar. He had been appointed guardian of the important baby. Bothwell arranged the journey in his capacity of Lord High Admiral. He did not accompany Mary, but Moray was now in constant attendance. The baby was left in Edinburgh Castle. Bothwell, appointed by Mary a captain of the Prince's bodyguard, remained at Edinburgh.

Mary began to plan for the baby's christening. The chief nobles and their men were to be dressed in special colours, decided by Mary. Bothwell's was to be blue, with silver and white linings.

Her thoughts were entirely on the coming ceremony. She dismissed from her mind the wrangling among her nobles and the rest, and recalled Secretary Lethington from the exile and disgrace in which his disloyal activities with Moray had placed him. He had played an important part in Moray's own rebellion, had fled over the border at the end of it, and had also given careful advice to the conspirators on the handling of the Rizzio murder.

But Mary could easily forget this sort of behaviour. Men were mortal, she declared, and had usually to be forgiven for whatever they did. Mary's main ambition now was to get her son recognised by Elizabeth as heir to the English throne. To obtain such recognition, she needed a subtle negotiator. The only man capable of this sort of work was Lethington. This was the reason she recalled him, whatever his loyalties might be at the time.

Bothwell was as much at enmity with Lethington as he was with Moray. Moray and Lethington were bosom friends. Mary organised one of her conciliatory dinner parties on Lethington's return. Moray, Argyle, Bothwell and Lethington attended. Lethington was delighted at her approach. Mary considered it a great success.

Bothwell repeatedly warned her that she was surrounding herself with potential enemies. Mary could not be bothered with such talk at the moment. She ignored him and she lived to regret it.

With the Queen fully recovered from the birth of the baby, it seemed advisable to do something about the situation in the Borders. Cancellation of the judicial progress planned by Bothwell before the birth had given encouragement to the troublemakers, who had looked on it as a sign of weakness. Although Moray was now constantly with the Queen, it did not seem very diplomatic to descend on the Borders at once. It would mean raising another small army. Mary did not want to start all that again. Everyone seemed reasonably friendly for a change: she had had enough of armies for the time being.

But assizes were normally held in the autumn. Perhaps she could attend the assizes, if they were held a little later than usual. This might serve the double purpose of reasserting her authority along the Border and preventing any more defections among the turbulent Borderers.

This was accordingly agreed upon and all the usual arrangements made. Moray and the others were to accompany her. Bothwell went on some days ahead to have everything in readiness. As Her Majesty's Lieutenant of the Borders, it was his duty to take up all the people due to appear at court and to put down any signs of unrest by capturing the ringleaders. The Hermitage became a prison on these occasions. Armstrongs, Elliots, and other troublemakers were rounded up: the heavy doors rumbled shut upon them until the day of the Jedburgh Assize. But one of the Elliots did not propose to hear this gloomy clanging. John Elliot, known as Jock o' the Park, took to the hills at Bothwell's approach. Outstripping his official escort, Bothwell came up to the galloping Elliot in a marshy dingle, where the

Kershope stream joins the Liddel Water. Cornered, the wild Elliot offered to come quietly if the Lieutenant would guarantee his life. That would depend on the verdict of the assize, Bothwell reminded him.

Elliot knew all about the type of 'Jedburgh Justice' dealt out by the Earl of Moray. It did not seem a healthy bargain. He leapt off his horse and darted away into the bracken. But Bothwell was ready for him. Pulling out a pistol, he brought Elliot down with a bullet in the top of the leg. Spurring forward, but finding the going boggy, Bothwell also leapt off his horse.

But, unlike Elliot, he fell flat on his face in the mud, almost on top of his victim. Jock o' the Park had not earned his reputation as a violent brigand for nothing. He wrenched the two-handed sword, for which he was famous, out of his belt and flailed his fallen pursuer with the clumsy blade.

It took more than a mudbath and a few near mortal blows to destroy the Hepburn. Before losing consciousness, he caught Elliot a couple of hard blows on breast and shoulder with his short sword. Jock lurched off into the undergrowth, dragging himself clear of the scene. Bothwell lay as if dead.

His escort soon came up. They piled his near-lifeless body on to a roughly made sledge and bumped him back along the moorland track. The Elliots collected their kinsman. He escaped the assize and eventually recovered.

But things had not gone well at the great castle either. All the Armstrong prisoners inside had overpowered their guards and made themselves masters of the Hermitage. It was an awkward situation for Bothwell's men. Had the Armstrongs known that Bothwell lay for dead beyond the castle moat, they would certainly have surged out and finished him off. Instead of this, they reflected on what would happen to them when the Lieutenant regained his castle.

Desperate to get their master in under cover and see to his injuries, Bothwell's men struck a bargain. In return for surrendering the Hermitage, all the prisoners inside should be allowed to go free, unmolested. They thankfully trooped home across the moors, while the Lieutenant was carried in to his bed. He was found to have three serious wounds, one on the left temple, one on the left hand, one in the side. He had lost a lot of blood and was still unconscious.

No one thought he would live. He was actually reported dead. The news spread like lightning through the Borders, to Edinburgh, to London, to Paris.

But the will to live was strong in the wounded man. He began to recover.

Meanwhile Mary had set off with Moray and the others to Jedburgh, where she had rented a small house in the town for forty pounds. The modest dwelling remains to this day, much as it was in October 1566. The assize proceeded normally, although the escape of all Bothwell's prisoners had reduced the number of cases to be heard.

As soon as the business was finished, and Bothwell was fit enough to have visitors, Mary determined to go over to the Hermitage. She had been heavily shocked by the news of his apparent death. To hear that he was going to recover after all sent her into tears of relief. The eighth day after the accident, Mary set out from Jedburgh with a large escort, accompanied by Moray, Secretary Lethington and the faithful Huntly.

She insisted on doing the return journey of some sixty miles all in the day. It is difficult to see why she thought such a taxing ride was necessary. With so many officials and other attendants there could have been no sense of impropriety had she stayed the night at the Hermitage. It is more likely that she knew the huge castle would be even more uncomfortable than Dunbar had been. To make sudden arrangements for her to spend the night with a great retinue would be a very large expense for her Lieutenant. In addition to this, he was still very ill.

Starting in the early hours, she reached the Hermitage safely. With Moray and the others, she sat round Bothwell's bed discussing the assize and making arrangements for the future. Bothwell was to complete the judicial business as soon as he was fit. Other items of local affairs were transacted, and the whole meeting reported to Cecil by a spy.

Mary then gathered up her escort and set off back to Jedburgh, where she arrived soon after five o'clock on a cold and dark October evening. As well as being tired, she was soaking wet. Her horse had come down in a bog along the hilly trail. She fell off and lost her left shoe and her watch. A sheep-farmer recovered these later, and they are now to be seen in her rented dwelling, incongruous in a glass case. The bog also survives, dignified by the name of The Queen's Mire.

But the mental and physical strain of the last few weeks had now overtaken her undaunted spirit. Racked with increasing pain from her ulcers and various unknown internal troubles, she collapsed. After a day or two of vomiting, fever and pain, she became still. Her body cooled and stiffened. Her eyes stayed closed. Her personal servants gently drew the curtains and opened the little window to allow her spirit free passage to the stars.

But shortly afterwards her eyes flickered open. Soft-slippered feet were padding gently round the room. Scooping all her jewellery, piece by piece, into a large leather bag, where it chinked on the silver and gold removed from next door, her dear half-brother, the Earl of Moray, was making a small private collection of her valuables. His apologetic smile, as her glistening eyes rested on him, can well be imagined.

Perhaps stimulated by this and by the superhuman efforts of her French physician and secretary, M Nau, who worked on her for three hours, Mary began to recover. After nine days, the crisis was over.

By 9th November, she was well enough to leave Jedburgh. Bothwell was also fit enough to come with her, in company with Moray, Lethington, and Huntly. They visited many of the Border strongholds and were well received, finally arriving at Dunbar by way of Berwick. Here the Warden, Sir John Forster, turned out the guns and troops to give her salute.

After staying at Dunbar, Mary went on to Craigmillar Castle, just outside Edinburgh, for a fortnight's convalescence.

She spent the time planning her next big occasion, the christening of her baby.

13

ON SUNDAY 17TH DECEMBER 1566, the little boy James was christened in the Royal Chapel at Stirling. Darnley refused to come to the service, and remained sulking in another part of the building. Bothwell assisted in the arrangements in every way he could, but refused to come inside the chapel during the service. He was still enough of a Protestant not to participate in a Catholic ceremony. Moray, Huntly, the Earl of Bedford, and other Scots and English Protestants also stayed in an anteroom while the ceremony was completed.

By his foolish behaviour, Darnley had now made known to the world in general his break with Mary. She had tried to encourage him, despite her revulsion at his private behaviour and his wickedness over Rizzio. With dignity she went through the long ceremony, and all the celebrations afterwards, without him.

But Darnley's time had not been spent entirely in the pursuit of pleasure. Big schemes were revolving in his mind. Nor was he alone. He could think now only of how he could be King, in fact, how he should be King, ruling the country with everyone obeying him. Mary had been unfair and unkind to him in not granting the crown matrimonial. And now she had this son, which would make things even more difficult. What was more, she was not a staunch Catholic like himself – at least, she was doing nothing to force the Catholic religion into every corner of Scotland.

He often spoke his thoughts aloud. People were apt to remember them, to pass them on. Surely there were powerful friends who would help him become supreme ruler, if only to see the old faith firmly entrenched? Darnley had an idea to go secretly across to Flanders, and meet Philip of Spain there. Afterwards, he would go to the Pope. They would all send a great army across to Scotland, and the French as well. He could lead them to Edinburgh where he, Darnley, would be crowned absolute King. The idea grew more and more attractive. He wrote to everyone concerned, discussed his secret plans with anyone who would listen. He gave secret orders for a ship to lie ready at Dumbarton to carry him to the Continent.

There was not much secrecy about all this. Mary asked him what was the meaning of stories about a ship lying at Dumbarton. He denied the story, but told her much of his plans for the full enforcement of Catholicism. Mary listened incredulously, unable to decide whether to believe him or not. Was he now going off his head, in addition to all his other drawbacks?

Other people were also discussing his secret plans. Chief among these were the Protestant leaders, Moray, Secretary Lethington, and the others. Darnley's plan would not suit them at all, if it were successful. Darnley must be removed from any position of influence, and all the nobles should now ignore him: that would solve the problem. From then onwards, Mary would become dependent again upon Moray's good counsel, and the whole situation would be restored to the position before her marriage. All good Protestants must sign a bond to disregard any orders or instructions the so-called King might give. Moray was pleased with this plan, and put it to Bothwell, with Lethington's discreet help, during a private conference in the Border country. Bothwell agreed in principle and gave his signature.

In November of that year, 1566, Moray's plan was carried a step further. Darnley must be divorced. Parliament would put this through to release Mary of the intolerable burden. In return for this, for which she would no doubt be most grateful, she could issue a pardon to Morton and all the other exiles, still banished to England after the Rizzio affair. The plan was put to the Queen herself. Bothwell had not signed the new agreement, although the divorce idea had been discussed with him during a stay at Craigmillar Castle.

Mary was dubious. As a good Catholic, there might be difficulties. The old consanguinity clause could not be invoked for fear of having her baby declared illegitimate. In view of her great interest in succession to the English throne, she could not risk this.

But she did not declare herself opposed to the general principle of parting company with Darnley. It was only the method about which she was doubtful. 'I will you do nothing,' she told Moray, 'whereto any spot may be laid to my honour and conscience.'

There were now several schemes in currency. Darnley's own Paris Plot, as it came to be called, did not look very hopeful. There was a rumour that Darnley himself was to be the object of some plot or other. His father got to hear that 'an enterprise to the great peril and danger' of Darnley was being planned. But no details arrived to support the story.

To Darnley's dismay, Moray eventually persuaded Mary to pardon Morton, who then returned to Scotland with all his fellow conspirators.

Bothwell spent his time between the Borders and Mary's Court. He retailed to her all the rumours as he received them. She either disbelieved or ignored the more sensational ones.

Anxiety and dissipation began to tell on Darnley. By the end of December he went down with a bout of syphilis, which did not surprise many people. He made an uncomfortable journey to his father's house in Glasgow, where he went straight to bed. Pustular sores broke out all over his body, his beautiful hair fell out in handfuls and his handsome face resembled the surface of the moon.

But this did not prevent his working on a new plan. He would go to Edinburgh as soon as he was well, destroy Mary, Bothwell, and as many of the others who got in the way, snatch up his baby, and declare himself unchallenged King of Scotland, either in Stirling or Glasgow. A few details needed working out. Who was actually to do it, and how? As he lay in discomfort in the darkened room, his new blue silk bedjacket round his pitted shoulders, various alternatives came to his fevered mind.

By 21st January, there was so much rumour and unease in the capital that Mary decided to bring Darnley back home. Bothwell

115

saw her safely to the outskirts of Glasgow, then returned to more judicial business at the Hermitage. He had spent a lot of time there recently. The Elliots and Armstrongs were by no means subdued. Bothwell had also been to Whittinghame, a place in East Lothian. He had a private meeting with Lethington, Morton, and several other Douglases. Morton later maintained that Bothwell had come to propose some mischief for Darnley. But there is no evidence for this. It is almost certain that Morton invited Bothwell to join him and the rest of the Douglases in their forthcoming schemes, and that Bothwell declined. Had it been the other way round, they would not have met at the Douglas's house. Bothwell mentions in his own memoirs that he was tired of adventures, imprisonments, and exile, and wished to settle down for a change. He was in favour of a peaceful divorce for Darnley. Morton may have asked Bothwell what Mary's opinion was now about a divorce, or even more stringent measures. Bothwell would have given the same answer for the Queen as on the previous occasion, when she had been asked the same question.

On 27th January, Bothwell was back in Liddisdale, dealing with a serious attack on his outposts and headquarters by the warlike Elliots.

A few days later, Mary had arrived back in Edinburgh, with Darnley. He was well enough to travel in a litter, but not yet fully recovered. Bothwell came to her shortly afterwards and stayed in his quarters at Holyrood.

The story of Kirk o' Field is well known, but the explanation has not always been clear.

Kirk o' Field was an old house standing on the site of the present Edinburgh University administrative buldings, about half a mile from Holyrood. It belonged to Robert Balfour, brother of the unsavoury Sir James Balfour who was captain of the troops at Edinburgh Castle. Darnley was strongly advised to move in to this house during his convalescence. He was said to have been suffering from smallpox in addition to his other ailments and needed to live apart from people until out of quarantine. Many advantages were put forward in favour of this house. It was in a quiet part of the city, the air was clean and fresh, and there was a nice garden just beside it. The house also had a honeycomb of vaults in its foundations.

Mary made preparations for him to spend the time at Craig-millar. She intended him to go straight there. After the quarantine, he was to come back to Holyrood. She started to make preparations in both these places. Only at the last minute did Darnley say he refused to go to Craigmillar, or direct to Holyrood, which Mary then suggested: he insisted on going to Kirk o' Field.

Mary gave in. She arranged for the removal of the new bed she had given him; it arrived only just before the invalid himself. A small bed of her own was also moved in. There were two main bedrooms. Darnley and his valet, William Taylor, slept in the upper room. Mary's bed was set up in the little room immediately below his. Although Darnley was still in quarantine, he had made a great point of Mary promising to spend at least two nights in the house, and also the last night of his quarantine, Sunday 9th February.

Everything went smoothly enough until Sunday evening. Mary went up to Kirk o' Field after supper, about nine o'clock, to spend the night there, as promised to Darnley. Bothwell, Huntly and one or two others were in the house with her. Moray had only that morning gone across to St Andrews. There was no sign of Secretary Lethington, nor of Morton. Darnley's father, Lennox, had left Glasgow the day before and come to Linlithgow, a few miles west of Edinburgh. No reason was given for this.

In the King's bedroom, Bothwell and Huntly gambled with dice on a green velvet tablecloth, together with Argyle and another friend. Mary sat beside the King's bed. Darnley was due to return to Holyrood the next day, his quarantine over. He was severely marked after his disease, and was still wearing the taffeta mask he had assumed to hide his face.

A couple of hours later, it was remembered that Mary had promised to attend a dance, which she was giving to celebrate the wedding that morning of one of her maids, Christina Hogg. Mary was very punctilious about fulfilling her promises. Although it was a very cold night with a powdering of snow, she insisted on going down to Holyrood.

Darnley was furious at her leaving and made most strenuous efforts to prevent her going: she had given her word she would stay that night. Mary was adamant, but promised to return to Kirk o' Field. She then gave him a ring off her finger.

With Bothwell and the rest of them, she set off to Holyrood, where she came in to the dancing. At about midnight, Bothwell and Traquair, Master of the Queen's Horse, drew her aside and were seen in close conversation with her. After about a quarter of an hour, Traquair left the room, leaving Bothwell and Mary still talking seriously together. Finally, the Queen withdrew to her room and did not return to the dance, neither did she go back up to Kirk o' Field.

Darnley went to bed after singing a Psalm with William Taylor, his valet, and drinking a glass of wine.

At half-past one there was a colossal explosion, which rattled almost every house in Edinburgh. Kirk o' Field had ceased to exist. Only rubble remained, and an outline of the foundations. In the little garden next to the house lay the near-naked bodies of Darnley and William Taylor, unscratched and without a mark on them. Nearby stood a chair. On the ground a clean dagger, Darnley's fur-trimmed dressing-gown, a shirt, a pair of slippers.

An agent of Cecil's was one of the first on the scene at daybreak. Nothing had yet been moved. He sketched exactly what he saw and sent the drawing off to Cecil. It survives to this day, the ink not much faded, all the details clearly visible and in good perspective. From this plan, the relative positions of the various walls and buildings can be studied. They are clear enough.

Over the years there have been many attempts to obscure the details of what happened that night. These attempts have mostly been successful. But now, fresh study has been able to establish beyond little doubt the extraordinary manoeuvres which culminated in this sensational murder.

Like many complicated plans, it only partially succeeded. There were meant to be other murders that night. Mary herself was on the list. Also Bothwell. Moray was to be a later victim. Also Morton.

It is only necessary to review the events of the weeks before the explosion to find the explanation.

The first plan was Darnley's own plan. He had chosen Kirk o' Field, in conjunction with Sir James Balfour, because of its useful honeycomb vaults. Sir James Balfour had bought ten pounds' worth of gunpowder in Edinburgh a few days before. He was able to do this without undue comment, because he was Captain of the Guard at the castle. With Darnley's connivance, the powder was stowed in barrels all through the foundations of Kirk o' Field.

Darnley's plan was to get Mary to spend Sunday night in her bedroom below his, and immediately over the basement vaults. Bothwell and several others of her entourage would also be sleeping in other parts of the house. Shortly before five o'clock in the morning, some of Morton's men, the Douglas family – Darnley's mother was of course a Douglas – would come to the house. Darnley had ordered his three 'great horses', recent gifts from Lord Seton, to come round to the side door at five o'clock. The fuse would be lit, Darnley would gallop clear, first to Holyrood, where he would collect the baby Prince, and then to Linlithgow to meet his father. Mary, Bothwell and some others would be dead. Darnley would naturally be made King and rule Scotland in Catholic splendour, helped by his good kinsman, Morton. Moray would be charged with the murder of Mary, from which the King had so mercifully been preserved, and would be executed.

This useful plan, as has been seen, did not succeed. It was foiled by Bothwell, although Morton was eventually beheaded for his complicity in the murder.

The next plan was Moray's. It was rather more subtle than Darnley's. Whereas the King's plan was ostensibly for the Catholic benefit, Moray's would be to the Protestant advantage.

Moray had made up his coolness with Darnley over the Rizzio affair, and the King had sufficiently overcome his fear of Moray to accept his friendship and company once more. Since Moray had again become such a close member of the Court and adviser to Mary, Darnley had not had much option. But for a long time Moray had nursed his revived ambition to be rid of Darnley. The warmth of his new friendship with the King was an indication of this. It was therefore natural that Darnley should share the arrangements for his own plot with Moray. Moray gave him every support and encouragement.

On the night in question, Moray established an alibi by going over to St Andrews. He knew of the details and is reported personally to have inspected the powder barrels before leaving Edinburgh. His plan was to fire the powder before the appointed time. A group of his men were seen hanging about the precincts of Kirk o' Field the whole of Sunday evening. Mary would be blown up – no one had anticipated her being away at Holyrood that night. Bothwell would probably be blown up as well. And Darnley would be blown up in the premature explosion. Moray would return in the early hours from St Andrews, collect the baby Prince into his care, and declare himself Regent, with the full and formidable backing of Elizabeth of England. Morton would be charged with the murder by the dead Queen's deeply grieving half-brother, who could not, of course, have been implicated in such a plot against his sister the Queen, whatever lies the accused Morton might produce at his trial.

After an interval, the young Prince, who was known not to be very strong, would pass away despite the best medical attention provided by the Regent. Who would then have an unchallengeable claim to the throne of Scotland? The Regent Moray would not shrink from this onerous duty if it were the people's wish.

This plan also failed. Although Moray did eventually become Regent, he was soon assassinated for the part that he did play in the murder.

Morton's plan was much the same, except for an important difference. Some of the Douglas family were to come up to Kirk o' Field in the middle of that same Sunday night and fire the fuse before the time prearranged with Darnley. Mary, Darnley and Bothwell would be blown up. Morton's men would dash to Holyrood, snatch up the baby and bring him to Morton, who would by then have reappeared from wherever he was hiding. Morton would then declare himself Regent. Moray would at once be accused of the murder, arraigned and executed. In return for being supported in his role as undisputed Regent, Morton would hand the young Prince over to Elizabeth's care. This would effectively remove the Catholic figurehead in Scotland, and discourage the continental Catholic powers from taking any action in Scotland.

It was an excellent plan, and was the one which came nearest to success. Had it not been for Bothwell, it might have succeeded.

The remaining details of what happened that cold Sunday night can no longer be doubted.

After the Queen had left Darnley at Kirk o' Field, intending to return after visiting the dance at Holyrood, Bothwell received definite information about a plot to blow up the house, while she and the King were asleep. It is possible that the bearer of this information was Bothwell's page, 'French Paris'. As the Queen had been leaving Kirk o' Field, Paris had appeared with his clothes very grubby. 'Jesus, Paris, how begrimed you are,' Mary is reported to have said at the sight of him. If this remark was correctly retailed, it indicates that Paris might have been down to the cellar to see for himself the truth of what he had just learnt.

It was clear to Bothwell that whatever had been planned at Kirk o' Field would have to take place that night, since both Mary and Darnley were to leave the next day to take up residence at Holyrood again.

There was therefore no time to wait until the next day and to investigate the matter more fully. Bothwell told Traquair, a captain of the Queen's Guard, and Master of the Horse, and between them they tried to persuade her not to return to Kirk o' Field.

Mary had given her word to Darnley that she would return. She had even given him the ring as a pledge of her promise. It was difficult to persuade her. After a long and serious discussion, she agreed to stay at Holyrood. But she did not agree to ride that night to Dunbar, for which purpose Bothwell had taken Traquair into his confidence. Traquair went to get horses made ready in the Holyrood stables and kept saddled all night, just in case they might be needed in a hurry.

Bothwell at last saw the Queen to her room and obtained her promise to stay there. He would go up himself, he told her, and see if the rumours were true.

Bothwell then went up to his own quarters and took off his festival suit of black velvet and satin, trimmed with silver lace. He put on his ordinary clothes, buckled on his sword, and threw his riding cloak about his shoulders. This was later remarked upon, because it was of the new 'English' colour.

Accompanied by Geordie Dalgleish, his servant, together with one or two more of his personal staff, he set off for Kirk o' Field. His passage through the city at dead of night was not attempted with any secrecy. For it has been claimed that Bothwell slunk out to fire the powder barrels which he had himself put in the cellar, and with his own men strangled Darnley, who had run out of the house, awakened by their arrival.

Bothwell went along the main street, the Canongate. He knocked on the city gates for admittance, giving his name, and being let in by the watchmen and gatekeepers at several points. This progress is well substantiated by many witnesses. It is not the action of a man going secretly to commit a murder in the middle of a sleeping city. On the way he stopped at an uncle's lodgings and called up for him to come with them. But the uncle, 'Black' Ormiston, was either too fast asleep to be woken by a shout in the street, or was not at home.

As Bothwell arrived at Kirk o' Field, it is well substantiated that one of the Balfour brothers, either Sir James, Captain of the Castle Guard, or Robert, owner of the house, was loitering nearby. Bothwell either asked him, or the information was volunteered, whether there was indeed powder in the basement. Whatever the reply, Bothwell went to see for himself. The Balfour would naturally have a set of keys for his own – or his brother's – house.

Bothwell then saw for himself the rows of barrels. The implications doubtless overwhelmed him. A few rapid inquiries brought out the news that Darnley's horses were ordered for five o'clock. It was unbelievable that such a plan should have been made. No wonder Darnley had made such a fuss about wanting Mary back in Kirk o' Field that very night. No horses had been ordered for Mary. And Bothwell himself might have been spending the night there.

In one of the moments of that instant decision for which he was so well known, he grabbed a tinder and lit the fuse himself. Impatient at the slowness of its burning, he went forward twice to blow on it. Each time he was pulled back by one of his men, on the second occasion in the nick of time to prevent his master being struck by the sudden convulsion of the building as the gunpowder exploded. He then made his way back to Holyrood, this time much more quickly and more directly.

All this noise, together with the muted clanking and whispering of Morton's Douglases as they gathered round in readiness to fire the gunpowder themselves, had woken Darnley. Looking out of his window, he could see the alleyway in which armed men were congregating. It was not possible to tell whose they were. He may also have got a whiff of smoke from Bothwell's efforts below. The doorway gave straight on to the men outside. He either realised in a second that his plan was being put into action without him or feared a murder attempt on his life. He knew he must get out at once. The window gave on to the garden. He could drop into the garden, dive through the conveniently sited doorway, and get into the safety of the orchard.

The window was not far from the ground, but anything would be a help to lessen the drop. He was still very much an invalid, and had not regained his strength. Darnley snatched up the small chair in his room, let it down on to the ground below his window, and slithered out himself on to the chair, which saved the last eighteen inches or so. He then scampered across the road and dived into the orchard.

But here the Douglases were also gathered. Darnley had doublecrossed them once before over the Rizzio murder. Now he was getting away before they could even doublecross him themselves. If he was to escape the explosion, at least he would not escape them. They caught hold of him. His terrified shriek rang out into the night. It was clearly heard and reported by several old women in the houses nearby, who had been wakened by the noise. 'Pity me, kinsmen,' they reported the next day hearing the King shout: 'Pity me, kinsmen, for the love of Him who saved the world.'

But the kinsmen had no pity. Darnley was expertly throttled in a very short time. It was suggested his shirt-tails were stuffed down his throat. Since no one who witnessed it provided this interesting detail, it has only superficial interest.

Very shortly after Darnley had got out of his bedroom window, the valet, William Taylor, clambered out. Thoughtfully, he carried his master's dressing-gown and slippers. The dagger, which was also found in the garden, may have been carried by Darnley, or could have been dropped in the dark by one of the Douglases. William Taylor ran after Darnley into the orchard. He met the same fate, only rather more quickly.

Who were Darnley's kinsmen? Only the Douglases, the men of Morton, came into this category.

Bothwell went back to Holyrood, took a draught of wine, and lay down in his bed.

123

At first light the city rang with the news. Bothwell was roused early by messengers. He was reported to have shouted, 'Fie, treason,' as he leapt out of bed. As Sheriff of Edinburgh, it was his duty to make all possible enquiries and establish what had happened.

14

MANY PEOPLE WERE taken up by orders of the Privy Council and tortured in an effort to establish the truth. Each unfortunate servant or citizen, who landed on the rack or in some torture chamber, gave whatever answers or explanation his inquisitor desired. Each faction of suspects had its own set of 'evidence' with which it incriminated the other.

Half of Moray's objective had been reached, although not by the means originally intended. It remained only to get Bothwell implicated and removed. Many stories began to circulate, many witnesses spoke of sayings and events which compromised Bothwell. Most of them, by constant repetition, have come to be accepted as fact.

But closer examination dismisses them all as patent absurdities, unsupported by disinterested evidence. One man said that Bothwell had brought powder 'in a large trunk' from Dunbar to Holyrood. He had kept it in his quarters there. Then the day before it had been taken on a grey cob, belonging to Bothwell, up the High Street to Kirk o' Field, all in broad daylight, and loaded by Bothwell and his servants into the cellars. One witness even claimed the trunk was too big to go in by the door, and that they had piled the powder loose on the floor, leaving the trunk outside. The story is too absurd to be taken seriously.

Another story is more vicious. It was aimed at implicating Mary and Bothwell jointly. It has been accepted as the truth for four hundred years, to the great wrong of both the Queen and her Lieutenant. All evidence is now against it. The story proclaims that Mary deliberately vacated her small bedroom below Darnley's that Sunday night. On the Sunday afternoon, Bothwell obtained a trunk of gunpowder, perhaps brought on the same grey cob, and had it carried up the narrow stairs into Mary's bedroom. Here it was tipped into a 'poke' or small conical pile on the floor. Knowing the powder was lying all over her bedroom floor, Mary declined to stay the night and went down to Holyrood on the pretext of having to attend the dance. Bothwell then went up and lit a fuse to the powder, which then blew up, killing Darnley. The explosion blew the King and his valet into the garden, where they were duly found.

Apart from the scientific fact that a loose pile of gunpowder in a room on the first floor could not possibly have destroyed an ancient stone-built house like Kirk o' Field, 'from the foundations to the roof', it would have been completely out of character for Mary to have been party to such a plot. In addition to this, the risks of discovery would be great. Someone would have remarked on the pile in the bedroom, even supposing it could have been introduced upstairs without anyone seeing it.

So-called confessions, either under torture or on the scaffold, are almost always worthless from the point of view of accuracy. In addition to this, so few people could write at all reasonably, that the chances of anything inconvenient being recorded were slim.

Moray and Morton, each probably in ignorance of what the other had intended for him, were now a powerful bloc again. They were determined to undermine Bothwell's position with the Queen and to destroy him. They would deal with the Queen and her baby afterwards. They would settle the question of the Regency later. Moray's claim was accepted as the strongest, since he had already acted so closely for Mary when she had first returned from France.

Bothwell in his official capacity retrieved Darnley's body and brought it back to Holyrood. It was laid, some busybody noted, on the same slab upon which Rizzio's corpse had been stretched. Darnley's, however, received a regal embalming at a cost of £42 6s 0d, which compares favourably with today's prices for the same service. Some three hundred years later, the chapel and burial ground fell into disrepair. Edinburgh citizens used the stones for their houses. Souvenir hunters dug up bones and other relics. At the end of the nineteenth century, an advertisement appeared in a paper offering one of Darnley's bones for sale from an address in Harrogate.

Mary was taken to see the body. She exercised majestic self-control and said nothing. What could she have said? Her silence at the sight of the body of the man she had once loved, whose son she may have borne, and whom she had come to revile, has usually been taken as evidence of her own guilty connivance at his murder. The fact that she left Kirk o' Field that night instead of staying as she had promised, is put forward to support the theory. Such pathetic substitutes for any real evidence of her complicity in a murder plot, together with all the other trumped-up charges against her, can be dismissed with the contempt they deserve. Apart from the lack of factual support for such allegations, even the most cursory study of her life shows any such connivance to be completely out of character. It would have been equally out of character for Bothwell to have devised a secret gunpowder plot.

But by the second week of March, the insidious campaign against both Bothwell and Mary had greatly intensified. People shouted in the streets at night that both were guilty of the murder. Posters were nailed up in prominent places during the darkness condemning them. Moray was undoubtedly responsible. Chief cartoonist was the same man, James Murray of Purdovis, who had suborned Bothwell's servant, Dandie Pringle, when Bothwell was in Paris. He had also been an active opponent of Bothwell's even at that time, retailing to Cecil all the gossip and slander he could find or make up. Murray pictured Bothwell as a hare and Mary as a mermaid with the letters MR and LB intertwined or displayed above swords and hammers. The allegory of hare and mermaid may have been clearer then than it is now. It was widely believed in England and on the Continent that Mary had been implicated, and that Bothwell had contrived the murder. Mary offered a reward of two thousand pounds with other money and a free pardon to anyone who would come forward with definite information. Bothwell hotly denied the murder, and, for his part, challenged to personal combat anyone who would accuse him to his face. No one took up his challenge. Bothwell went about with a powerful and numerous bodyguard.

One of the effects of the campaign against Mary and Bothwell was to bring them closer together. Mary was now back in the situation of having no one else to comfort or advise her. She went with Bothwell to Seton.

During this time, Moray, Morton, Lennox, practically everyone else, whether Catholic or Protestant, had combined in an effort to bring Bothwell to ruin and to incriminate the Queen. The sight of Bothwell now conducting the affairs of the country, with Mary at his side, was more than Moray or Morton could stand. It was the situation in which they each saw themselves. They decided that Lennox should demand a public trial of the people who were being so vociferously accused. Bothwell agreed at once to stand trial, confident of acquittal. He made no effort to intimidate the court, the jury was one chosen in routine fashion and the Lord Chief Justice was still the Earl of Argyle, brother-in-law of Moray. He knew there was no evidence to convict him of murder. He had suspected Murray of Purdovis to be the cartoonist who was achieving such notoriety. He obtained a warrant for his arrest, but Murray was nowhere to be found.

Cecil instructed the Earl of Bedford, in the name of Elizabeth, to produce as many witnesses for the trial as could be persuaded to testify to Bothwell's disadvantage. Cecil saw a new opportunity of getting rid of Bothwell, isolating the Queen, and restoring Moray as a puppet regent.

There was much interest abroad in the trial, which was fixed for 15th April. During preparations for it, Mary bore up very well. It was an anxious time for her. She was not unmoved by the murder, and spent many hours in prayer. Mass was sung in the Chapel Royal in Holyrood by her special instruction. For this occasion, Mary had some of the sacred lengths of cloth of gold, taken from the English tents at Bannockburn in 1314, cut into strips and used for decoration. Three of the best bits she gave to Bothwell. It is not reported what he did with them. They had been kept in veneration at Aberdeen: many people were incensed at this use of the relics of Scotland's distant victory over England.

Lennox was not prepared to trust to the normal course of law and justice to obtain the verdict that was so essential to him and his new associates. As the day of the trial grew near, he assembled a force of over three thousand men at Linlithgow, ready to escort him to Edinburgh. But Bothwell already had experience of bringing armies to court-houses. Moray had packed the court the day Bothwell had been due to stand trial for breaking gaol: Lennox was not going to get away with the same intimidation. Lennox was told that six attendants was the limit allowed by a plaintiff at such a court. Arriving at court with any more than this would be treated as treason and contempt.

Lennox sent urgently to Moray for advice. But Moray had left the day before, going down to report to Cecil before crossing to France. He was far too cunning to be present at what promised to be a rumbustious trial of uncertain outcome.

Lennox dissolved into panic. He hurried back to Stirling. From there he wrote to the Queen asking for a postponement of the trial, since he was now ill and could not travel, and also had not had time to prepare the case. Until such time as he could be ready, he demanded that Bothwell and the remainder of the accused's associates should be put in prison.

His complaints and requests were ignored. The court met at noon. Bothwell arrived from Holyrood in a throng of militant supporters. A servant of Lennox answered in the name of his master asking for the postponement. But the court, having noted that it was not long before the trial that Lennox had been demanding immediate action against the accused, decided that there were no grounds for postponement. Consequently, no one appeared to put the case against Bothwell. By seven in the evening, their verdict came out. Bothwell was completely acquitted of all charges and declared innocent of all complicity in the murder of the King.

Before the court had dispersed, a messenger was on his way to Lennox with the verdict. Rather than await a visit from Bothwell, who might have wished to discuss the matter further, Lennox hurriedly got on to a boat at Dumbarton and sailed down to England, where he was met by his wife.

The trial had not been a success for Moray, Morton, Lennox or for any of Bothwell's opponents and Mary's enemies.

But to Bothwell's annoyance, it did not finish the matter. The secret campaign of vilification, instead of coming to an end, was intensified. More and more posters appeared, ignoring the verdict of the court and naming Bothwell and all his servants, friends and associates as the murderers.

Bothwell again issued a general challenge to anyone still inclined to accuse him. This time the challenge was accepted, anonymously, suggesting the contest should be decided in England or France.

This was an intolerable situation for Bothwell and very disquieting for Mary. The next meeting of Parliament was three days after the trial. At the ceremonial opening, Bothwell carried the sceptre before the Queen. It was an anxious time for both of them. But as he later wrote in his memoirs, Parliament completely ratified the verdict, and forbade anyone to continue to accuse or harass him on that account. The sticking-up of slanderous posters was also strongly forbidden. The public were instructed to pull down any they saw.

Other measures were passed. But, although momentarily in a position of power, Bothwell never arranged for huge benefits for himself, as Moray had done on previous occasions. There is merely a record that the grant of property round Dunbar Castle, together with the castle itself, which Bothwell already enjoyed, should be reaffirmed in his ownership. Two small properties were granted to David Chalmers in recognition of his faithful service to Bothwell in exile. Beyond these, Bothwell took nothing for himself.

At about this time, Bothwell decided on a step which would be the logical outcome of his career. He would marry Mary himself. He had no reason to suppose Mary would not agree. His devotion to her was deep-seated. It had been put to formidable test over the last few years. He had never wavered in the face of imprisonment and exile. His recent experiences and close association with her led him to believe she would give her consent.

But she would wish to know that the majority of the nobles of her realm would be in agreement. For this purpose, before mentioning his plan directly to Mary, Bothwell gave a dinner-party at his quarters at Holyrood, the night Parliament broke up. Twenty-eight of the principal nobles and men of the Church who were available accepted his invitation. There is no substantiation for the allegation that it was no more than an uproarious feast in the back of a public house in Edinburgh called Ainslie's Tavern. It was the nearest equivalent to a State banquet, without the presence of the Queen.

It is customary to maintain that at the end of the dinner,

Bothwell astonished the company by suddenly producing a document, to which he invited their signatures. The document laid out the circumstances of Bothwell's recent trial and acquittal. It went on to declare that the Queen should obviously take a new husband, both for the comfort of herself and the benefit of the country. Should her choice fall upon that nobleman who had served her so well and earned her affection so truly, the Earl of Bothwell, then all those present wished to record their hearty approval. They could think of no one more suited to be consort, bearing in mind his innumerable good qualities, and would do everything in their power to support and uphold the marriage.

Such a document certainly was produced. But there is no evidence to show that it came as a surprise to his guests. There was no discussion. Everyone willingly signed, except the Earl of Eglinton, who slipped away before being handed the pen. It is declared that the signatures were enforced by the near presence of a large body of troops. But Bothwell would not have employed troops in an effort to force a signature. It would not only have been almost impossible to do, but would openly have given the lie to his contention that everyone present was in wholehearted and voluntary agreement with the proposal. One of the signatories was Morton. Moray was still out of the country.

It has further been suggested that such a marriage proposal was seen by Bothwell's opponents as clear proof of Mary's and Bothwell's guilt. If they actually got married, then it would be evident that they had engineered the murder in order to get married.

But it was well known that Mary could have divorced Darnley. His murder would make marriage with Bothwell no easier than it would otherwise have been: in fact, it could make it more difficult, since suspicions would have been made greater. Had Mary so desired, she could have married Bothwell without having recourse to murder, which was anyway alien to her nature.

The next day, Bothwell joined Mary at Seton, where she was resting. In a letter to her usual correspondent, the Bishop of Dunblane in Paris, she herself describes what happened next. It seems that Bothwell was not in his most tactful frame of mind. Her secretary described an incident, when some of the soldiers of the Guard burst in just as Bothwell was about to broach the delicate question of marriage. They had not been paid for two months. Bothwell struck their spokesman for his impudence, and a brawl developed. This was a poor start, but he persevered when the room had been cleared. Mary wrote: 'He began afar off to discover his intentions unto us and to essay if he might by humble suit purchase our good will . . .' but he obtained 'nothing correspondent to his desire'. Mary was in no mood at the moment to consider marriage, even when shown a document which declared that many of her nobles and Churchmen thought it would be a good idea.

But the idea had been put into her head. It may have been there already.

Mary went off to see her son at Stirling. Bothwell, according to a letter on Cecil's files, left her, declaring he would be raising a force for a sweep through the Borders during the next day or so. But Bothwell did not go down to the Borders, or anywhere near. He went to Calder Castle, a massive place some twelve miles south-west of Edinburgh. He had nearly eight hundred horsemen with him.

Two days later, Mary left Stirling to return to Holyrood. The violent pain to which she was occasionally susceptible overwhelmed her on the journey, and she spent the night at Linlithgow, after an emergency stop at a cottage by the roadside. Huntly was with her. It was reported, but not proved, that Bothwell rode over to Linlithgow that night and spoke for over an hour with his brother-in-law, Huntly, without seeing the Queen. He then returned to Calder, where he was reported to have been 'in great ill humour'. Any interpretation of this incident must be conjectural. Whatever was said, if the meeting transpired, must have had a close bearing on what happened the next day.

As Mary rode along the track from Linlithgow, Bothwell suddenly came up and took her bridle. Behind him appeared his eight hundred men. Mary's escort on her private journey was under forty strong. There was great danger ahead, he declared. Mary should come at once with him to the safety of Dunbar. Mary agreed. She had no reason not to believe him.

But one of her attendants, James Borthwick, did not believe him. He offered to ride at once to Edinburgh, sound the alarm and get help. Mary sent him on his errand.

When he got to Edinburgh, he was so certain in his disbelief that he reported the Queen had been kidnapped and must be rescued. The provost at once had the bell rung and sounded a general alarm. In a very short time, a number of citizens had taken up warlike positions. Two guns, more mobile than the rest, were pushed out of the castle armoury, loaded and fired off at the cavalcade, which now appeared trotting eastwards past the city. It was more of a gesture than anything else. Bothwell and his troops paid no attention, and the citizens gave up.

The party did not reach Dunbar until the middle of the night. Mary again described what happened in a letter to the Bishop of Dunblane. Bothwell renewed his proposal of marriage. Mary at first was no more inclined to agree than she had been at Seton. She even protested to Bothwell at her treatment, and accused him of being ungrateful to her after all she had done for him. He talked with her for most of the rest of the night. According to Mary, he went over his whole life's history, told her how deeply he loved her, and complained how unfairly he had been hounded by so many 'unfriends'.

It is clear that she was greatly sympathetic towards him. Her sympathy did not at that stage extend to marriage. But during the next day or two, her opinion rapidly changed. Her breath had been taken away by his audacity, now she knew there had been no special danger. Huntly and Secretary Lethington were with her. They quarrelled and went home separately. Melville the diarist, also with her, did not know what to make of it all, and spent the time scratching notes for his diary. Mary had no one to help her make decisions. No one came forward to ask if he was needed. As usual, no one lifted a finger to help her. But she may not have been in need of help.

She had arrived on Thursday. By Saturday she had decided that marriage to Bothwell would be the best thing after all. She had always admired him. He was brave, vigorous, decisive, and ruthless. She had seen all that. The more she thought about him, the more she began to wonder whether she was not falling in love with him. Also, she realised she was for the time being completely in his power.

The Bishop of Dunblane received all her thoughts in her letter. 'In the end,' she wrote, '. . . we were compelled to mitigate our displeasure and began to think upon that he propounded.'

Perhaps Bothwell would be just the man to help her rule unruly Scotland. At times she had been so exhausted that she had prayed for some strong right hand to help, guide, and guard her. She was, she told the Bishop, 'already wearied and almost broken with the frequent uproars and rebellions raised against us since we came to Scotland'.

Many stories have been told of what happened between Mary and Bothwell during those crucial three days. The most popular and scurrilous story, excitedly repeated for generations after, was that Bothwell raped her in that cold draughty room at Dunbar.

There is no evidence of this. Although it was not unusual for servants to be present during intercourse in those days, there has been no word of any witnesses of such an event. The story was concocted by those who wished to extract Mary from any suggestions of voluntary alliance with Bothwell, and to blacken Bothwell. Had he, in fact, raped her, it is suggested she would have been obliged to marry him. Bothwell did not have to do this to win her consent to marry him: she stated quite clearly that she agreed to marry him after much careful thought, not as a result of being assaulted.

None of the people, who gleefully reported at the time that he had raped her, could possibly have known whether it was true, unless they had witnessed it themselves, or been told by one of the two concerned.

There remained the fact that Bothwell was already married to Huntly's sister, Lady Jean Gordon. But on the same Saturday that Bothwell and Mary were at Dunbar, Lady Jean started proceedings for a divorce.

This implies that Bothwell had been closely in touch with his wife beforehand about the possiblity of a divorce. He may have mentioned to her that he was hoping Mary would take him as her husband, and that divorce arrangements should be put under way. As soon as Mary had agreed to marry Bothwell, Lady Jean started her petition. Huntly, her brother, had already given his consent. It is doubtful whether all these arrangements could have been made in the space of one day.

Lady Jean put her case before the Protestant court on the

grounds of her husband's adultery the year before with one of her maids, Bessie Crawford. It is curious that this incident, which, with other similar ones, very possibly did occur at Haddington and other places, did not precipitate divorce proceedings much earlier. Lady Jean doubtless had her reasons for doing nothing about it for twelve months. Bothwell's lawyer entered a refutation and denial, presumably as a matter of form, but Lady Jean obtained her decree.

Bothwell himself applied to the Catholic court for his marriage to be set aside. There now appears an interesting problem. Bothwell applied for a decree of nullity of his marriage on the grounds of consanguinity, or too-close relationship. But he had obtained from the Pope, before he married, a special dispensation to allow him to marry her despite this prohibited degree of consanguinity.

What is the explanation of this? Lady Jean kept the original dispensation, depositing it in the charter room at Dunrobin, when she later married the Earl of Sutherland. The document can be seen there to this day, as has been mentioned already. Bothwell knew about that dispensation, because he applied for it himself. Did Mary know of these dispensations?

There was even confusion among the Churchmen at the time. For the day after Lady Jean had applied to the Protestant court, the Primate of Scotland appointed a commission of six, including two bishops, to enquire into the whole affair of his marriage. The Bishops could not decide what to do. Eventually they declared that Bothwell's marriage had never been legal, whatever dispensation had been obtained. He was therefore quite free to marry again.

After the initial confusion about the legalities of his previous marriage, Bothwell and Mary began to take up a life more normal for a Queen and her consort elect. They appeared together in public more cheerfully clad. The usual activities and pastimes of Court life began to occupy their days. The Privy Council met and transacted business. It looked as if the uproar and scandals of the previous month or two had given place to a more ordered routine.

But at Stirling, matters were by no means being allowed to rest. Morton and his associates, who now included the Earls of Mar, Atholl, Argyle, and others, planned a violent disruption of the new-found peace. They were actively advised by the absent Moray, now in France, through a stream of couriers and supported by constant messages from Cecil and Elizabeth's envoy, the Earl of Bedford.

Word reached Bothwell of their schemes. He planned to set up the first regular army in Scotland, a body of troops permanently on call. This would have been a great feature in establishing some form of order in the country. But it came to nothing for lack of money.

By 6th May, Mary and Bothwell were ready to return to Edinburgh. They had been at Dunbar for ten days. With a strong force, they entered the city without any demonstrations being made against them. Bothwell led her into the city, himself on foot at her horse's head, accompanied by an unarmed escort. They lodged in the castle for greater security. The loyal commander of the castle was now Sir James Cockburn. But mysteriously, Bothwell relieved him of his command and gave it to that despicable traitor, Sir James Balfour. It has been suggested that the only reason for this could be blackmail by Balfour, who may have threatened to declare that he saw Bothwell light the fuse and thus cause the explosion, which most people thought had killed the King.

But before taking any serious military action against the threatening body of dissidents in Stirling, Bothwell was anxious to get the wedding arranged and over. To the annoyance of Mary and Bothwell, the minister of St Giles Cathedral refused to call the banns. He even came to Holyrood, to which they had now moved, and harangued them on their alleged adultery and other misdemeanours. He was lucky to get away with such impudence. The Church overruled him and the banns were called.

But the minister was not alone in his opinions. Stimulated by troublemakers from the Stirling headquarters, there began to be public mutterings at the prospective marriage. Mary quietened these by appearing herself before a large gathering, including representatives of the Church, the State, and the Law. She declared her mind was freely and voluntarily made up to marry Bothwell. In this she foresaw much good for the peace of the realm and perhaps, at last, a little peace and personal happiness for herself. He was entirely forgiven for any appearance of having acted against her will, as were all those who had associated with him in any way.

To demonstrate her regard and affection, she created Bothwell Duke of Orkney and Lord of Shetland, titles which his family had once held.

By 14th May, all the formalities had been completed. The marriage contract was signed at last. Secretary Lethington was one of the witnesses. Typically devious, he had remained voluntarily with Mary, protesting to the Stirling Lords that he was held a prisoner, quite unable to return to them. They did not believe this. But Lethington was not accustomed to being believed and paid no attention.

Preparations for the marriage went forward. The ceremony was arranged for the following day, 15th May 1567.

15

THE WEDDING TOOK place early in the morning in the great hall at Holyrood. It was a Protestant service and well attended by all except the Stirling rebel ringleaders. A great banquet was held afterwards, to which the public were admitted as spectators.

It was not considered seemly to hold a fiesta as had been the case at Bothwell's and Mary's previous marriages. Mary did not wish to create an impression of undue gaiety so soon after the death of Darnley. This was very understandable, whatever her opinion of him had latterly become. Bothwell was content to spend as much time with her as he could. It is not surprising that Mary was reported to be in a very emotional state after the wedding. On top of her natural emotions on such an occasion, her unstable health had been severely taxed during the past few weeks. Fits of heavy weeping and depression were not unnatural for her at any time. When they occurred now, it was pointed out that she must be desperately unhappy about the marriage.

There is no adequate evidence to support this. She was often seen affectionately on Bothwell's arm. There were also reports of scenes and rows between them, with Mary threatening to kill herself and calling for a knife. His enemies complained he was 'so beastly jealous and suspicious that he suffered her not to pass a day in patience ... He would not let her look at anybody, or anybody look at her ...' Some girls would be glad to see their husband of a few days being so possessive. Bothwell had additional cause for wishing to protect her. He could never be sure that reports of a plan to snatch her out of his keeping and take her to Stirling were no more than a rumour.

Mary wrote fully to her Catholic contacts abroad, explaining how she had come to take Bothwell in marriage and to hold the ceremony according to Protestant rites. Bothwell in his turn told Mary almost all he knew about Darnley's murder. There is no evidence to show that he had not already discussed this with her nearer the time. But it was probably only at that stage that she realized how her half-brother and his friends had plotted to destroy her. Her grief would have been great. Her relief at having Bothwell at her side through it all would have been redoubled.

Great play has been made with the fact that at her wedding with Darnley, Mary gave him unending quantities of furs, satins, rich stuffs for doublets, cloaks, caps, carpets, and feathers of all descriptions. Yet to Bothwell she gave only a fur tippet of her mother's to edge his dressing-gown.

But what would Bothwell have wanted with satins and feathers? Her greatest gift she had given him, the gift of herself. They were both now deeply in love. They had no need of dainty presents offered between them.

They had need of a more serious commodity in short supply – loyalty to the sovereign. If Bothwell and Mary had been given the support by the rest of the country to which they were fully entitled, Scotland would have started a new era of economic and political stability, which would have transformed the next century. In the short time allowed them together, many most useful acts were passed dealing with all manner of the country's affairs. The judiciary, Parliament, and the law offices were reorganised. An air of efficiency and purpose began to be reflected in the papers and orders which survive from those few weeks.

But it was not a pleasant prospect for the scowling traitors slinking round Stirling. Morton and his cronies were enraged at the bustle in public affairs created by the new rulers. Moray, from his safe distance, fulminated against the diversion of revenues from his bursting coffers to the public service.

Bothwell took a vigorous hand in all public affairs. The marriage contract had stipulated that all documents were to be signed jointly by the Queen and himself. There could be no suggestion of self-benefit for Bothwell, unlike his predecessors in the role of Regent or Consort. He wrote to the French explaining his position. He told Elizabeth of England how much he hoped she would revise any poor opinion she might have held of him. He would work for the closer association of the two countries, which he said, he knew to be her aim also.

But time was running out for the new régime. The Stirling rebels were getting restless. Bothwell thought it wise to counteract any move from that quarter by assembling a force at Melrose, and possibly moving up against the rebels.

Summonses went out for all loyal men to gather at Melrose on 15th June, when the Queen and her husband would review them. The Queen issued a statement that no new steps were being anticipated by her: that, contrary to rumour, she was not thinking of sending her son out of the country. It had been an idea of Bothwell's to have the baby Prince brought up in France, but nothing of that nature was contemplated.

Ominously, Secretary Lethington defected suddenly to the rebels on 6th June, without saying goodbye to Mary. The Queen was very put out, especially as Bothwell had had words with Lethington shortly before. Lethington, as machiavellian as ever, sneaked into Edinburgh Castle to confer with Sir James Balfour, to whom Bothwell had given command of the castle.

For three hours, it was reported, they talked and plotted. The outcome was an undertaking by Balfour that he would turn the castle over to the rebels as soon as they arrived, in order to help them release their Queen from the detention in which Bothwell was supposed to be holding her. Lethington pledged himself to support Balfour in his claim to retain command of the castle, whatever the outcome.

Curiously uninformed by his normally efficient intelligence service, Bothwell set off with Mary to Borthwick Castle, on the way to the Melrose meeting. Had he known what the rebels were planning it is unlikely that Bothwell would have left the capital. But this was not the first time that his spies had let him down before a crisis. There was the Rizzio plot, of which Bothwell had been ignorant until the murder took place.

As soon as he was clear of Edinburgh, Morton and his men moved in behind him. They were watching him closely. Like fox and geese on a draughts board, his every move was covered. He was getting nearer and nearer the corner.

The night he reached Borthwick, Bothwell went on with some

fifty men to Melrose, leaving the Queen at Borthwick. Such was the propaganda which Morton had built up throughout the country against Bothwell and the Queen that no one had responded to her call to arms. Melrose was empty.

This was the first sign of real trouble. It is possible Bothwell was not surprised at the failure of the muster. He knew how much work had been put in on the Borders by Morton during his exile. During the last few months, Morton's men had been going up and down the country, stirring up disaffection. But Bothwell will have hoped that his marriage to the Queen might have quietened opposition.

His hopes were ill-founded. The very night he got back from Melrose, a thousand horsemen, with Morton and Kerr of Cessford among them, nearly got into Borthwick by pretending they were friends. They then ringed the walls like Red Indians, shouting threats and challenges to Bothwell, and screaming abuse at the Queen.

Bothwell was delighted at a chance to do personal battle, but the Queen would not allow him. She herself stood on the wall shouting bravely back at the mob, which must have looked thousands strong in the half-light.

It was the first time that Mary had felt the weight of public indignation and false hatred against her. It was not the last. She was astonished and disbelieving at the turn of events. She still longed for a general conciliation, for some way of turning the people's inexplicable anger from her into love, loyalty, and affection. She sent two men with messages for Huntly, back in Edinburgh, asking for help. Morton's men captured them both, but released them after holding them all night. The messengers got through to Huntly who immediately roused the city. But second thoughts overcame his initial surge of duty. The city was still partially occupied by Morton's men. And the castle was in the hands of Morton's ally, Sir James Balfour. The city decided to do nothing, and Huntly was powerless.

Bothwell resolved to slip away from beleaguered Borthwick, out into the open where manoeuvres would be unrestricted. Dressed as a woman, with one man accompanying him, he stole out of Borthwick. His companion was taken at once, but Bothwell got away to Haddington.

The next night, learning that Bothwell had got out, and not wishing to lay siege to the Queen in her castle, the troops withdrew to Edinburgh.

As soon as they had gone, Mary, in men's clothes, left Borthwick. Bothwell was waiting at nearby Cakemuir Castle. In the gaunt room still known as Queen Mary's Hall, she changed back into her own clothes. Together they rode again to Dunbar, arriving in the small hours.

As the dawn came, they lost no time in sending out a proclamation in the name of the Queen for all able-bodied men to come to her aid at Dunbar. First to appear was the Provost of Dunbar, who offered his loyal support. He was offering his loyal support to Morton at the same time, but may not have mentioned this.

Morton was also issuing proclamations, inviting support. He had better luck than the Queen. He had the capital in his hands, and a large and rapidly-growing body of troops. To Mary, very few came. It was difficult to know what to do, whether to march against Morton, to build up a bigger army at Dunbar, or perhaps to sail for France to get help.

On Morton's side, the first enthusiasms began to fade. In their hearts, none of the soldiery wished to march against their Queen. And no one was very anxious to start a battle with the Earl of Bothwell. Perhaps they should disband and let things sort themselves out through time. It looked like stalemate, or a collapse of the opposition.

But with his final act of supreme treachery, Sir James Balfour provided a solution. In consultation with Morton, he decided on a plan to draw Bothwell and the Queen out from Dunbar into the open.

He sent her a message to say that the moment was ripe for her to march on Edinburgh. She could be assured of the guns of the castle: once it was known that the royal army was approaching, he said, opposition would vanish and her authority would be established once more.

This seemed to make sense. Bothwell collected all the troops he could muster, including pathetically few supporters from the Borders and round about. He and Mary then led this small army out in the middle of the morning for the march on Edinburgh.

There were under three hundred men. Two hundred of them were Bothwell's arquebusiers, and sixty of them part of the regular mounted guard. But by the time they got to Haddington the number had grown encouragingly to six hundred cavalry. By evening they were at Prestonpans, sixteen hundred strong. Mary and Bothwell went down into Seton House for the night.

They were optimistic about the outcome of their advance on Edinburgh. They dined with Lord Seton who had always been a faithful friend. They spent their last night at the house which had so often given them hospitality. They never dined together again.

Now the rebels had recovered some of their resolve. They had been joined by a contingent from the north. Feeling more confident, they left Edinburgh at two o'clock on Sunday morning and marched towards Dunbar. Morton's general idea was to destroy Bothwell, take the Queen into protective custody and get himself, or perhaps Moray to begin with, established as Regent until the Queen could be married more suitably. They halted at Musselburgh, a little town six miles along the road. According to witnesses, they made an early breakfast, not renewing operations until after seven o'clock.

By this time Bothwell had also got his camp on the move. He came up with his troops to Carberry Hill, just east of Mussel-burgh. He had reconnoitred the ground in approved fashion and selected the higher ground to have the advantage over the rebels. He had field guns well positioned: the rebels had none. He had superiority of terrain. The sun was behind him. His cavalry were disciplined and efficient. He had with him the Queen of Scotland. Had his forces stayed firm in the face of the rebels, he would surely have won and held the day.

The rebels were still doubtful of what to do. There was unease at the prospect of bearing arms openly against the Queen. A sketch made on the spot at the time still survives. It shows the chief weapon of the rebels boldly displayed. This was a huge banner with a naked figure lying prone over an apple tree. Beside it a child could be made out, crudely drawn. The words printed above could clearly be read by anyone who could read: no doubt there were plenty to help the illiterate. 'Judge and revenge my cause, O Lord,' the child prayed on his knees. This banner appeared to upset Mary and Bothwell's troops. In addition, the day became hot and they had no midday meal, an early engagement being expected. To Bothwell's fury, his men began to drift away in small parties to the village to look for food and to wander along the hill behind to fill their waterbottles. Bothwell wished to attack at once, but Mary would not allow it. Her horror of bloodshed was with her always.

A small group eventually came forward from the rebels, encouraged by the French Ambassador, du Croc. He had made strenuous efforts to patch up the quarrel: Morton was adamant that his army would disband only if Bothwell was either rendered up or went away, leaving the Queen in their charge. Du Croc reported Bothwell's much-quoted retort, a valiant, defiant and dignified challenge to the forces of treason and rebellion ranged before the Queen. 'What harm have I done them?' he thundered. 'I never wished to displease any, but have sought to gratify them all. Their words proceed from envy of my favour. But Fortune is free to any who can win her.' His final shaft would have struck firmly home. 'There is not a man of them but wishes himself in my place.'

The Queen, reports the Ambassador, turned to Bothwell with tears in her eyes. Bothwell offered at once, as he had offered before, to lay his life at risk for her sake in a personal challenge to any one of the traitors of noble birth who would come forward. He urged du Croc to get someone to take up the challenge. 'If you do', he urged the Ambassador, 'you will see a fight well fought'.

The sporting element introduced by the Queen's champion was not received with enthusiasm. Mary herself caught at Bothwell and told him she would never consent to such a contest. 'I am bound to acknowledge,' wrote du Croc, 'that the Duke seemed to me a great Captain, speaking with undaunted confidence and leading his army gaily and skilfully. For some time I took pleasure in watching him and judged that he would have the best of the battle if his men stayed faithful.' But even while the parleying was going on, the Queen's men were dwindling fast. An eye-witness estimated there were barely four hundred of the two thousand left. 'I admired him when he saw his enemies so resolute: he could not count on half his men and yet was not dismayed. He had not on his side a single lord of note. I rated his chances higher because

144

he was in sole command. I doubted that the other side had too many councillors: there was great disagreement among them. I took my leave of the Queen with regret,' wrote the Frenchman, 'and left her with tears in the eyes of both of us.'

James Murray, the spy, insolently put himself forward. Sir William Kirkcaldy of Grange, the chief rebel General, then offered to accept Bothwell's challenge. But, said Bothwell, he was neither earl nor lord, but a baron, and so was not his equal. Lord Tullibardine then offered himself but was similarly rejected. Since they seemed to be having some difficulty in suggesting a name, Bothwell himself issued his challenge direct to Morton. The chief rebel accepted and chose broadswords as weapons. But when he noted the eagerness of his friends to push him forward and hold his sword and armour ready for him to put on, he had second thoughts. He was prepared to shout insults at the Earl of Bothwell. To stand before him alone with only a sword in his hand was another matter. Lord Lindsay was Morton's great friend. The friendship was put to the test when Morton turned to Lindsay and awarded him the honour of accepting in Morton's name. Melville, the diarist, notes that Lindsay 'then offered to fight, which he could not well refuse. But', continues Melville, 'his heart failed him and he grew cold in the business.' But his name had gone forward and he had to start making preparations. He delayed them endlessly.

Bothwell waited and waited for his opponent to appear. The afternoon wore on, the sun went round behind the rebels to shine straight in the face of the royal squadrons. By now there were barely two hundred left round the Queen and her loyal husband.

Lindsay never appeared. Instead, the rebel army began to gather itself up as evening drew on. Flanking cavalry moved out right and left. The central body of infantry bestirred itself and moved slowly forward.

Kirkcaldy of Grange came forward with another message for the Queen. Leave your husband, he urged, and come over to us for discussions. This way there would be no bloodshed. The Lord Bothwell shall be free to ride unmolested from the field. He, Kirkcaldy of Grange, General of the Confederate forces, would personally guarantee her safe conduct and return to Edinburgh. To Bothwell another note was handed. Leave now, it said, and you will leave in freedom. But stay, and no one will answer for your safety, so great is the hatred against you. Bothwell warned her at once that it was nothing but a trick. She must not trust them. Far better to turn back to Dunbar and plan another campaign. Bothwell tried his hardest to persuade her. But she insisted on taking the rebels at their word, in trusting them as she had trusted so many people before.

The Queen spoke for several long minutes aside with Bothwell. She was seen to cling to him in floods of tears. What they said will never be known. It is not difficult to imagine. Throughout history, what more noble, dramatic and tragic moment has ever hung upon the evening air?

The whole encampment was still: all eyes were upon the Borderer in his glinting armour, in his arms the Queen of Scotland in her scarlet tunic. Again and again they kissed. As they parted, he was heard to ask if she would remain his faithful wife to the end. All the company round heard her promise to do so.

At long last, he turned and strode to his huge black horse. Beckoning to a few of his men around him, he trotted over the rise to the east, out of her life and into history.

Bothwell rode straight to his castle at Dunbar. He was not pursued. No one dared molest him.

Mary fared worse. As he had predicted, the rebel Lords broke their word at once. She was dragged in a mob to Edinburgh. Dusty, tear-stained and barefoot, her clothes in ribbons, she was hauled into what was no more than a cupboard, with a window on to the main street of Edinburgh. No woman was allowed to her. All night they hooted and bellowed outside her window, lit fires which flickered against the wall, screamed insults and threats until dawn.

Before she collapsed, her untamed spirit brought her to the window in the view of them all. If the Lord were willing, she would crucify them all and raze their city to the ground.

So ended the fine promises of Sir William Kirkcaldy of Grange, General of the army. So also the word of honour of James Douglas, fourth Earl of Morton, and of others of his ignoble band.

16

BACK IN DUNBAR CASTLE, Bothwell began at once to make new plans. The first essential was to see what support could be raised to rescue the Queen. She had promised in those few awful last moments to remain true to him. He was heard to have asked her, and her reply was equally clear. Had she not promised this before, swearing that she would follow him to the ends of the world in, if need be, nothing but a white petticoat?

The Queen had now been forced on to a jaded pack-pony and dragged all the way to Loch Leven. On either side, wrenching alternately at her bridle and brutally urging her on, were that evil man, Lord Ruthven, and Lord Reres, himself reckoned to be little better than an animal. In the castle, in the middle of that windswept lake, she was locked in a small corner room. Her gaolers were the Douglases, Darnley's kinsmen. Chatelaine of this tiny keep was Lady Douglas. She had been one of James V's innumerable mistresses. Moray was their son, born before James married Mary's mother. In Lady Douglas's opinion, her son Moray should have been king.

The orders from Morton were to kill the Queen if any rescue attempt was made. When the news of these instructions came through to Bothwell, he realised that any local and immediate rescue would be too dangerous to her life. He decided on longer-term arrangements.

On 20th June, five days after the disaster at Carberry Hill, the rebel Lords promised a reward of one thousand crowns for anyone who would deliver Bothwell to them. There were no takers.

Bothwell was undeterred by offers of rewards for his capture.

Leaving Dunbar in the hands of his local friend, Patrick White-law, he went by boat across the Firth of Forth into Fife. From there he went on westwards to Linlithgow, in the heart of enemy country. One of the Hamiltons here promised him support. He left then for Dumbarton on the west coast, which Lord Fleming was holding for the Queen, despite violent threats from Morton. Queen Elizabeth's Ambassador now reported to Cecil that Bothwell was building up quite a volume of support. He himself wrote that some fifty people of importance had rallied to him in support of the Queen.

By 25th June, Bothwell was back in Dunbar, weighing up the possibilities of getting sufficient support to usurp the rebels and restore the Queen with safety. The next day found him in the Borders assessing support in the traditional Bothwell country. The Kerrs of Ferniehurst promised all they could, together with several other leading families. The same night Bothwell was back in Dunbar.

Serious news came through to him. Many of his servants and friends had been taken by the rebels. Most had been tortured to 'confess' all manner of deeds, nearly all conveniently implicating Bothwell in the murder of Darnley. Some even involved Mary herself. All the stories, obtained under such duress, have little if any value. The unfortunate victims were reported to have said what their torturers wanted to hear, with suitably 'natural' variations. One of the most notable of Bothwell's servants to be caught was Geordie Dalgleish, at one time tailor to his master. To save himself from the extremes of torture, Dalgleish led his captors to a small silver box which he said his master had sent him to fetch. Inside the box were, it was given out, the letters and documents which formed the basis of the notorious Casket Letters. There were various innocuous papers in it, nothing approximating to the reams of letters used later by Morton and others in the well-known attempt to incriminate Mary and Bothwell in Darnley's murder. They were never produced in public in their entirety, and never produced at all to Mary for her to refute them, although she constantly demanded this elementary right. The so-called Casket Letters are now seen to have been a particularly clever and cunning ragbag of forgeries, interpolations and genuine letters from Mary, Anna Throndssen and others.

Poems alleged to be Mary's could never have come from her pen. This could easily have been proved had they been put on show. Morton hung on to the complete folio of forgeries until his death.

The rebels now had Moray as Regent, newly returned to Scotland. He was determined to eliminate any trace of Bothwell: he soon had him declared an outlaw and all his possessions and honours forfeited. This would attach to anyone found helping or harbouring him. With Moray now in a position of such power, there was nothing more Bothwell could do. On 27th June, he left Dunbar for the last time. Patrick Whitelaw, who had been knighted on the same day as Bothwell received his Dukedom, held the castle against all comers until 1st October. This was not before he had been completely blockaded, and the whole battery of siege guns from Edinburgh Castle brought over to range against him.

Bothwell went by boat again up the east coast and arrived at Strathbogie in Aberdeenshire, the home of his former brother-in-law, Huntly. But Huntly realised it was a hopeless cause. He could now hold out no hope of support towards re-establishing the Queen.

Bothwell's movements during these few weeks have not yet been clearly made out. It is not anyway of great importance. But when he is next heard of, he is back with his great-uncle, the Bishop of Moray, at Spynie. The old man had followed his career with sympathy. He was always assured of a welcome there. But this time, things were not so pleasant. Some of the Bishop's illegitimate sons fell out with Bothwell as he planned his next move.

The English Ambassador, Throckmorton, throws a little light on the Spynie episode, when no other source bears upon it. The Bishop's tenants had been ordered by the Council in Edinburgh to withhold their rent from the Bishop because of the shelter given to Bothwell. This was a good reason for the friction which ended in Bothwell leaving Spynie. There was an additional complication. An English spy held by the Bishop got word to Throckmorton that he was party to a plot, presumably laid by the illegitimate sons, to murder, or at least take, Bothwell, and anyway to murder the Bishop. He asked what should be done with Bothwell. But Throckmorton declined to involve the

English Court at that late stage of developments, doubtless thinking that Bothwell was not enough of a menace now for Elizabeth to get implicated. The English purpose was now well served, with Bothwell in eclipse and Mary imprisoned.

But before he left, Bothwell discovered the brothers' plot, in which the English spy had been invited to co-operate. He soon put out the sons and their friends and took over Spynie himself.

His new plan was to establish a fleet and start from there. As Hereditary Lord High Admiral of Scotland, he was in a good position to organise this. Whether he proposed to turn it into a pirate fleet, of which he had been accused on former occasions, or whether he had the idea to build up a naval force for use in a landing, is not clear.

But his first prey was a boat belonging to Moray, which he found lying off the coast. This was soon relieved of its cargo of food and annexed. He describes how he chartered another, a twin-masted ship called the *Pelican*. She belonged to a Hanseatic merchant called Captain Gerhard Hamlin, trading from Bremen to the Shetlands. The *Pelican* was taking on cargo at Sunbergh Head. The merchant readily engaged her to him for the next two months, for fifty crowns a month. Bothwell agreed to pay sixteen hundred crowns compensation should the *Pelican* be lost or not returned at the end of the charter, or should he wish to buy her. For the artillery on board the charge was one hundred crowns. Bothwell adopted her as his flagship. He then took on another ship belonging, as he thought, to another merchant from Hamburg. Unknown to Bothwell, this second merchant was no merchant at all, but a pirate captain called David Wodt, who had himself illegally seized the vessel on the high seas. This fact was not realised in Shetland, and Bothwell chartered her in good faith. Before long he had collected half a dozen ships. Moray became alarmed. When he had been returning from France to take up the Regency, he had visited Queen Elizabeth. She showed him some ships which she said she would fit out and send against Bothwell. But nothing came of this, nor was it probably intended.

On 10th August, Moray ordered the Dundee authorites to fit out any available ships they had, to sail against Bothwell. Nine days later, four ships were ready altogether, the *Unicorn,* the *Primrose,* the *James,* and the *Robert*. Four hundred arquebusiers were put aboard, as well as cannon, and Kirkcaldy of Grange and Murray of Tullibardine went aboard in joint command. Also in the party was the Bishop of Orkney who had married Mary and Bothwell.

It was hoped that Bothwell would now finally be taken. Lethington, who had re-emerged among the rebel hierarchy after his defection from Mary, told Throckmorton that 'they had good hope of Bothwell shortly'.

The fleet of four sailed straight for the Orkneys.

Bothwell had been in the Orkneys for a couple of days. The islands were delighted to receive their new Duke. They offered him help of all sorts and entertained him in their homes. There was a notable exception. This was the Sheriff of the Orkneys, and custodian of the two main castles of Noltland and Kirkwall. He happened by bad luck to be Gilbert Balfour, a brother of the treacherous Sir James to whom Bothwell had given the coveted command of Edinburgh Castle. Gilbert refused to help and even ventured to fire on Bothwell's ships as they sailed under the lee of Kirkwall's fortifications. It was not worth Bothwell's while to invade these strongholds. He had with him about two hundred men and, as he says himself, about forty gentlemen. It was a useful party, but not large enough for any undue risks to be taken. He therefore sailed on to the Shetland Islands for a more secure base.

Bressay Sound runs inland, sheltered from the wild North Sea, yet studded with rocks and reefs. Bothwell's ships dropped anchor. Here again the new Lord of Shetland was warmly received. This time there was no sheriff or custodian wishing to deny him entry. Bothwell rowed ashore with many of his men, leaving his ships standing out in the Sound. A meal of welcome was quickly prepared by Olaf Sinclair, who was the bailiff, the equivalent of sheriff.

Bothwell and his closest supporters sat down to the luncheon soon after midday.

Before the meal was halfway through, shouts came echoing across the water. Into the mouth of the Sound came the *Unicorn*, the *Primrose*, the *James*, and the *Robert*.

Such a sudden pursuit had been quite unexpected. Gilbert Balfour of Orkney was doubtless to blame for setting the ships so

151

promptly on Bothwell's trail. There was no time to get back on board. Acting on their instructions for such an emergency, the *Pelican* and her three sister ships slashed their anchor cables and ran north before the fortunate breeze still blowing. The Sound narrowed to the north, before giving to open sea again. On board all his vessels were local pilots. The *Pelican* flew on, a rapid sailer. The others did their best to catch up. But one was a sluggard, seaworthy but slow. The island records still tell the details. On the great *Unicorn,* pride of Scotland, Kirkcaldy of Grange could be seen standing in the prow, shouting and urging on his ship. Beside him stood the now warlike Bishop of Orkney, his purple robes billowing over a heavy suit of armour.

The *Unicorn* came creaming through the water under all sail. Bothwell's little ship also had run up all sail, but her canvas looked pathetically small against her pursuer. At the helm was a Shetland fisherman. He knew the draught of his ship. He knew the great rock which lay like a submerged whale just below the surface in the centre of the channel. Straight for the rock he steered, and scraped across. The triumphant *Unicorn,* poised for the capture, had a draught of thirteen feet. The rock lay eight feet below the surface. The crack of shivering timbers and splintering wood could be heard inland. She burst asunder and sank. In another moment the heavily armoured Bishop would also have gone to the bottom. Likewise many of the crew and perhaps Kirkcaldy of Grange as well. But the *Primrose,* the *James,* and the *Robert* were all at hand. They put about at once and the *Unicorn's* complement was rescued. But Bothwell's ships were out of sight, including the slowest which had lured the *Unicorn* to her destruction. The rock bears the name Unicorn Rock to this day.

They went on to the far north of the Shetland Islands and put in at the island of Unst to wait for Bothwell. Before long, crossing the various sounds and islands, he arrived and picked up his vessels. Owing to his hurried departure from the luncheon table, some of his men had got scattered. Kirkcaldy of Grange, eventually put ashore, spent the time looking all over the islands for anyone he could find. Bothwell must have debated whether he would not settle accounts with the treacherous Kirkcaldy. But with only two hundred men of his own, and some of these still on the other ships, he may not have thought it worthwhile. But when he joined his ships at Unst, he sent one back along the west coast to the Bay of Scalloway to collect the men whom he had not been able to gather up. As soon as they returned, he put to sea again.

By this time the *Primrose, James,* and *Robert* had appeared once more on the near horizon. Bothwell had decided to put off from Shetland, perhaps to run to France or Holland, or even Denmark, to see if continental support could be raised. But Tullibardine in the *Primrose* was determined to come up with him. With no more friendly rocks at hand, the victor of the *Unicorn* was at a disadvantage. She was soon caught. The other two sailed on into the gathering night. They suffered severely from the guns of their pursuers, being themselves only armed to ward off pirates, while the other three were warships. Making use of every navigational ruse, the wounded *Pelican,* her main mast snapped, her hull holed and many men killed by shot, kept ahead. Her escort dodged time and time again from assault and boarding. Both ships lost ground and began to answer sluggishly. Tullibardine thought to have the prize at last, although it is doubtful if Bothwell would ever have been taken alive. They were estimated to be sixty miles from Unst by now, and the distances closing rapidly.

But as darkness gathered, a gale sprang up out of the west as if in answer to the Lord High Admiral's prayer. With each gust the waves rose and the spume flew in a veil around the *Pelican* and her one remaining escort. Visibility fell away. Tullibardine dropped further and further back and finally gave up.

On and on into the night on the wings of the storm, the valiant Duke of Orkney sailed his battered force.

Morning dawned calm. The horizon was clear of pursuit. To the east a faint land mass was visible. Bothwell recounts in his memoirs how he came up with a merchant vessel from Rostock on the Don. The captain agreed to help them make landfall at the nearest harbour. They could patch up their ships, reprovision them, and carry on to whatever place from which Bothwell had intended to seek help.

The tongue of sea reaching inland where they made the coast was Karmesund. The Rostock boat helped them make fast. As they prepared to relax and put things shipshape, fresh troubles arrived. They had not reached the coast unnoticed. Captain Christian Aalborg, of the Royal Danish Navy, was on patrol against pirates along the Norwegian coast in his cruiser, the *Bear*. Norway belonged to Denmark at the time, ably ruled by Frederik II by whom Bothwell had been well entertained when travelling to France. Captain Aalborg was naturally inquisitive, suspecting that he had come upon one of the privateers then so frequently conducting private voyages of piracy all over the North Sea.

It was difficult for Bothwell to explain that he had no papers, having had to leave in the face of rebellion. To have to add that the Queen of Scotland was captured and a prisoner made the story sound unlikely. To begin with, Bothwell writes in his memoirs, he did not disclose his identity. Dressed in torn old clothes, well patched, he did not, at first sight, look like the Lord High Admiral of Scotland and husband of the Queen. The battered and demasted *Pelican* did not look like a ruler's flagship. The Danish captain could be forgiven for deciding that the vessel with its complement must accompany him to Bergen to establish the alleged credentials. By a simple ruse, the Dane invited some of the *Pelican's* men on board the *Bear*, together with more from the remaining Scottish ship, on the pretext of offering hospitality. As soon as both Bothwell's vessels were then made inoperative, the Dane announced that the whole party was under arrest on suspicion of piracy, and would be taken down the coast to appear before the Danish ruler of Norway, Erik Rosenkrantz.

Had Bothwell decided, immediately on seeing the *Bear,* to take matters into his own hands, he could probably have overwhelmed Captain Aalborg and his detachment. He had about one hundred and forty men with him. But he had no idea that he would not be reasonably received, once he stated who he was. Also a direct attack on a Danish man-of-war would have branded him as a brigand and would have forfeited any sympathy which he hoped to gain further south.

Boarding parties were therefore put aboard the *Pelican* and her escort, and the three ships set sail for Bergen.

On 2nd September they sailed into the harbour of Bergen. This trading port was the seat of the Danish Overlordship of Norway. Rosenkrantz occupied the fort still known as the Rosenkrantz Tower. News of the arrival was brought to him. He at once sent a party of merchants and citizens aboard to investigate. Although mystified at the lack of credentials and of appropriate clothing of the self-declared late ruler of Scotland, they returned satisfied that here was no pirate in a stolen vessel, but indeed a man of importance, who had met with various adventures to account for his being in such curious straits. When asked why he had no authority or credentials to pass out of Scotland, Bothwell says he replied: 'Who can give me credentials? Being myself the supreme ruler of the land, of whom can I receive authority?'

There had been some awkward moments when three of Bothwell's servants denied knowing who he was. This could not have been true. They even mentioned that their ship belonged to Wodt, the known pirate, which gave the Scottish party, for a short space of time, an impression of disreputability in the eyes of the law-abiding and God-fearing merchants. But all the explanations seemed satisfactory as far as they went. Rosenkrantz was uncertain what to do about his obviously very eminent uninvited guest.

He had not been very happy about letting such a large party land in the middle of the town. But on receiving the report, permission was given for Bothwell to take rooms in an inn. Bothwell then issued a statement to say that he had perfectly good answers to any questions which anyone wished to put to him. His ships were legally acquired under contract. The *Pelican*, in particular, had been recognised by some acquaintances of its owner among the other Hanseatic traders who happened to be at Bergen.

For the rest of September, Bothwell stayed in Bergen, not as a prisoner, but not as a free man either. He told Rosenkrantz that he wished to pass on to visit Frederik II and other princes, and would be glad to be allowed to proceed.

He might well have got away before, had not a further stroke of ill-luck come upon him. By amazing chance, Anna Throndssen appeared on the scene. Anna, who had patiently followed him about so long during the early years, who had pawned all her jewels and possessions to help him, and given him all the money she could when he had nothing, the Anna whom he had installed in one of his towers on the Borders and seemed completely to have forgotten. Rosenkrantz was a cousin of hers. She arrived in Bergen for a family wedding. What astonishment must have been hers to find the man whom she hoped for so long to marry, and who appeared to have lost all interest in her, under house arrest in a hostel in the town! Once more, and supremely, Anna could have helped the man she must once have loved. An effort from her at this stage would have raised Bothwell up from the predicament he was in, perhaps restored to him the chance of many years more of happy and useful life on the Continent – perhaps even as her husband at last. But in Anna, the milk of human kindness had not only turned sour: it had curdled. On Bothwell, now apparently friendless, destitute and a prisoner, she turned her venom. She raised an action against him for the return of all the money she had given him nearly eight years before. To this action, she added complaints that he had jilted her, taken her from her home and family on promise of marriage and not fulfilled his bargain. She produced in the courtroom handfuls of letters, proving, she said, that she was entitled to compensation.

Bothwell made no reply to her jumble of charges. He merely offered her a pension of one hundred marks a year from some unspecified source in Scotland, and the gift of the smaller of his two ships. The *Pelican,* of course, now reverted to the owner, under his contract. Hanseatic agents would have seen to that as she lay in Bergen harbour.

Had Anna's one-time undoubted love for Bothwell endured just a little longer, Rosenkrantz would almost certainly have withdrawn his restrictions over him. Bothwell would have gone free once more. What then might have happened when he turned his face once more to Scotland, as he surely would have done? The signpost reading 'If only . . .' stands at the junction of all roads of history. This is one of the most intriguing – and profitless – to follow.

Anna had made it impossible for Rosenkrantz not to take further notice of Bothwell.

At this juncture, the smaller vessel was about to be delivered to Anna. Bothwell had said he had nothing on the boat he ever wanted to see again. But just before the handover, he said that, after all, there was a small case hidden below the boarding which he would like to have.

This was fetched and opened in front of Rosenkrantz. Had Bothwell been allowed to open it first himself in the privacy of his room in the inn, matters might have turned out differently. For in the case was his deed of appointment to the Dukedom of Orkney signed by the Queen, as well as a letter from her to him in her own hand, complaining of the treatment she had received and how no friends had stood by her. So she had been able to keep in touch with him even after the disaster at Carberry Hill.

But in addition to these, there was a copy of the Commission to Kirkcaldy of Grange and Tullibardine to arm and equip ships to take him on the high seas, or wherever they might find him. Also a copy of the general proclamation declaring him murderer of the King and an outlaw, with the price of one thousand crowns on his head, dead or alive.

This was another disaster for Bothwell. If only he had left the case to rot in the bilge of Anna's little ship!

This was now a different matter for Rosenkrantz. He felt the responsibility was now too much. Bothwell must go down to Copenhagen for the authorities to decide what action should be taken.

On 25th September, he received Bothwell sumptuously in his official residence. On the 28th, he threw a huge banquet in honour of his illustrious, but now departing visitor. Two days later, with only four or five of his servants, Bothwell was on his way in His Danish Majesty's vessel, the *Bear,* to Copenhagen. The flame of hope and freedom which had flared briefly in the Scandinavian gloom began to die.

Rosenkrantz gave the use of a small two-masted vessel to those of Bothwell's faithful company who wished to return to Scotland as their master sailed away. Towards the end of December they were driven ashore on the Orkneys and seized. Lord Robert Stuart, Moray's other illegitimate half-brother, had quickly made himself Lord of Orkney as soon as Bothwell had left. Into his hands the gallant company fell as they staggered off the cliffs in the storm.

The third ship of Bothwell's small fleet, which he had sent to the Bay of Scalloway to pick up the men scattered by the arrival of the *Unicorn* in Bressay Sound, had followed the *Pelican* across to Norway. They had dropped anchor in Bergen harbour, some time after the *Pelican* had arrived and Bothwell had been placed under house arrest. Before they could leave their vessel and go on board the *Pelican,* they realised that all was not well, and that they themselves were liable to arrest. The anchor was hardly down when they hauled it up again and put straight out to sea. On board were all the remains of Bothwell's personal belongings which he had been able to take with him away from Dunbar. His armour, some jewels, some plate with his crest newly put on by the Queen's silversmith before their wedding, were on board. They never came back to Scotland, nor did word ever come through of what happened. They may have gone down, been taken by pirates, or put in secretly to some little continental port. Perhaps somewhere in the water, a jewel of the Lord High Admiral's sparkles in the light, on the wall of some castle or museum a piece of armour glistens, on some neon-lit shelf a piece of plate gleams, bearing the crest of a bridled horse's head.

17

AT THE BEGINNING of October, the *Bear* arrived at Copenhagen. The King was away in North Jutland. His steward, Peter Oxe, was instructed to put Bothwell securely, but comfortably, in the castle. The Copenhagen records, which fully detail these events, record the steward's anxiety at being responsible for the safe-keeping of a figure with such a reputation as the Earl of Bothwell's. He sent the King a report of all that had led up to the Earl's arrival. Enclosed with this was a letter to the King from Bothwell himself, together with a translation attached by the steward.

Bothwell also wrote to Charles IX of France, seeking help for Mary and for himself.

But other people were also writing letters. Back in Scotland the Regent Moray was smarting at the way Bothwell had eluded him. He wrote to Frederik of Denmark as soon as it was confirmed that Bothwell was detained in Norway. He demanded that the prisoner should be surrendered and sent back to Scotland for trial. Although written on 25th August, this letter was not delivered to Frederik until the middle of December. The bearer of the letter excused the long delay by blaming the weather. Even then, it was a long time to take from Scotland to Denmark.

Frederik was not inclined to take instructions from Moray about his prisoner. He declared he was not convinced that Bothwell was guilty of anything which required his extradition. There was anyway a judgment of the Scottish Council completely exonerating Bothwell from any blame in the murder of the Scottish King. Moreover, he pointed out, Moray was himself in rebellion against his rightful Queen. There was perhaps a Danish equivalent of the phrase about the pot and the kettle.

But all the same, Frederik agreed it might not be convenient if Bothwell disappeared. He therefore gave instructions, which can still be read today, to the Captain of the Castle at Malmö, across the Sound from Copenhagen. '. . . Have the vaulted room prepared . . . wall up the closet in the room and where the iron lattice of the windows is not strong and quite secure, have it repaired. When the Earl arrives, put him in the room and give him a bed and good entertainment . . . Before all things, keep good watch and ward on the said Earl, as you may best devise, that he does not escape.' Today the vaulted room is still there in the now much-altered castle. The closet remains clearly walled up. The remaining iron lattice looks strong and quite secure, not in need of repair.

In this fortress, Bothwell dictated his story of some of the events leading to his presence at Malmö. It was written in French; the present author has turned it faithfully into English.

Bothwell campaigned skilfully for his release in the face of Moray's repeated attempts to have him extradited. Moray even sent the notorious mercenary, Captain John Clerk, across with instructions to get permission to execute Bothwell himself. Needless to say, Frederik paid little heed to such an impudent request.

Bothwell now played his trump card. It did not take the trick, but it kept the grisly game in play for ten more years. In return for his release, Bothwell said to Frederik, he would cede to Denmark the islands of Orkney and Shetland, which he was empowered to do by virtue of his own patent of the Dukedom. If this were acceptable, he would undertake that Queen Mary of Scotland would sign the necessary document to set the full seal upon the bargain.

The islands had originally belonged to Denmark. They should still have done. Frederik was intrigued.

But by now, additional pressure was upon him to deliver up his prisoner. Queen Elizabeth and Cecil also concocted letters to Frederik urging extradition. Every excuse that could be thought of was put forward. Send him to England, if not to Scotland. She

1 See page 165.

assured him that Bothwell would have fair trial. But Frederik still demurred.

On 2nd May of the same year, 1568, one of the greatest stories of the time reached its electrifying climax. Mary escaped from Loch Leven Castle.

But before the special envoy could reach her beloved husband with the news, the light that so briefly and brilliantly lit the scene had gone out. All had been lost at Langside for lack of a general. Bothwell would never have lost that last battle, had he only been free to command her forces.

On 16th May she was rowed across the Solway. Those few steps up on to the deserted Cumberland quay were the last free steps she trod.

Mary's political collapse and detention in England forced the crisis in Frederik's mind. Mary's cause was obviously lost. In return for permission to recruit some two thousand Scotsmen for the war against Sweden, he would deliver Bothwell for trial in Denmark or Scotland. But first he would sound the opinion of other rulers, after having received the mercenaries. The notorious Captain John Clerk, a mercenary himself, was to collect Bothwell, or cut his head off and bring that back, if nothing better could be done. Frederik paid little attention to this mean envoy.

Clerk only brought back two of Bothwell's young servants, William Murray and the page Nicholas Hubert, often called 'French Paris'. Under torture they produced completely unreliable stories of their master's implication in the Darnley murder. Before taking Murray and 'French Paris' away, Clerk had met a naval captain, Peter Adrian, from Sussex, commanding a Danish ship. Adrian lodged with Murray. Clerk encouraged Adrian to visit Bothwell with Murray and get to know what Bothwell was up to, if anything. Adrian sent a detailed account of his conversations back to Cecil. It survives today among the vast library of Cecil's documents.

Adrian's comments are of the greatest interest, being some of the few first-hand records of Bothwell's speech to survive.

Frederik made a kindly allowance to Bothwell of money for clothes and general upkeep, without any word of repayment. A regular order for silk and velvet was given to a merchant at Odessa for Bothwell, for which Frederik paid.

Bothwell was at this stage by no means rigidly confined. Although under strict house arrest, he received letters and visits, and wrote to whomever he liked.

Most interesting of all, he corresponded regularly with Mary. None of their letters has yet been discovered. But Bothwell was kept well posted of events in Scotland. He very soon heard of the murder of Moray in January 1570.

The Earl of Lennox, Darnley's father, became the next Regent. He made renewed efforts to get Bothwell extradited. He nearly succeeded. He sent a more cunning envoy, Buchanan, to try once more to persuade Frederik.

It was Buchanan who complained that Bothwell and Mary should not be allowed to correspond so freely. He discovered the couriers and urged their detention. They were an Englishman called 'Master Horsey', and a Danish page called Herman. This latter was an exceptional character. Buchanan complained that he regularly 'came forth of Scotland and entered in England at the East March, disguised in his apparel, passing on foot in a blue coat, a blue Scots cap on his head, and a fork on his shoulder, as the common custom of the Northern people is to go'. His particular value was in being able to speak Scots so well as to be taken for a Scotsman.

At this stage Frederik agreed to give Bothwell up. Only the intervention of Charles of France once more prevented this.

But the sands were running out now. The Catholic massacre of Protestants on St Bartholemew's Day destroyed all possible sympathy for a Catholic Queen to return to her throne. With this, no one would now raise a hand to organise anything for Mary's relief. With Mary's was coupled the fate of Bothwell. Although Frederik, for fear of what the neighbouring rulers would think of him, and for his general humanitarian views, still refused to hand Bothwell over, he withdrew all his privileges such as the supplies of velvet and silk. On 16th June 1573, he sent Bothwell to the castle of Dragshölm, a pleasant but well secured castle above the water in North Zealand.

In 1575 reports began to circulate that the Scottish Earl had lost his reason. No one denied them. For Frederik, Bothwell had become an embarrassment. At Dragshölm, the Earl had a certain amount of liberty within the castle walls. He was still in touch with Mary, which is known from chance remarks in Danish documents.

In Scotland, the old pattern of violence continued. In September 1571, Lennox was ambushed by a party of men still faithful to the Queen, led by Bothwell's brother-in-law, the Earl of Huntly, and Lord Claude Hamilton. Captain Calder killed the Regent with a pistol shot.

The Earl of Mar took over. In October of the next year, he died of poison. Finally Morton became Regent at long last. The Queen's men were now a greatly diminished band, but led surprisingly by Kirkcaldy of Grange and Maitland of Lethington. Were they hoping to atone for their unending treachery and betrayal of their Queen at a time when their loyalty might have saved her life and career? They held Edinburgh Castle for Mary against Morton, surrendering only in May 1573. Kirkcaldy was hanged, Lethington committed suicide by poison.

With the surrender of Edinburgh Castle died the last vestiges of support for Mary Queen of Scots. Her country, to which she had devoted her adult life, for better or for worse, washed its hands of her.

Away in Denmark, her faithful husband paced the ramparts and courtyards of Dragsholm Castle. Morton made one final effort to lay hands on him. In June 1575 he wrote reminding King Frederik's steward that the King had promised extradition in return for the right to levy the mercenaries. He complained the promise was still not fulfilled. Morton also tried to get Frederik to release Captain John Clerk, the mercenary, who had overstepped the mark and also landed in Dragsholm. Later that year Clerk died.

In 1573, Bothwell's mother, the Lady of Morham, died. In the same year died the old great-uncle, the Bishop of Moray, at Spynie.

Before his removal to Dragsholm, Bothwell became ill at Malmö. He is alleged to have written a confession, the text of which survives. It is now known to be a complete forgery. Even the names of some of the supposed witnesses are those of people known by that date to be dead.

It is possible that the severe head wound he received from Jock o' the Park in the days of his greatness on the Borders gradually affected his brain. It is clear that latterly he slipped away into the realms of unreality, no longer being able to take his usual walks around the high walls of the castle overlooking the fjord. His fierce spirit would not have taken kindly to detention.

At last on 14th April 1578 he gave up the struggle – the first he had ever given up. Nine years later, Mary joined him in eternity. They had kept faith together, as they had promised on Carberry Hill. Mary never broke the marriage. No sovereign ever had a truer servant, and no woman a better man.

The Last Word

THIS IS A translation of Bothwell's own version of what happened during the last few years.

Its authenticity is unquestionable, unlike many of the stories and documents about him.

It is not a very good story: it is not even very accurate. It is certainly not the full story. It may be a poor thing, but it is his own. It is what he wanted to say, and he said it. There were no ghost writers or clever friends at hand to help him make it sound better.

It is only right that it should be read.

It was dictated by Bothwell in French to a Danish secretary appointed to the task by the Swedish King Frederik. The subheadings, which appear in the margin in the original, were in Bothwell's handwriting.

Les Affaires du Comte de Boduel

Matters concerning the Earl of Bothwell, 1568

To enable the King of Denmark and the Council of his Kingdom to get a better and clearer idea of the wickedness and treason of those who are accusing me, whom I list below, I have laid out truthfully and as concisely as I can the causes of the troubles and commotions which have occurred from the year 1559 up to the present day. These people have been the chief authors of them all.

I have likewise made known their slanderous behaviour towards me, and all the great wrong and injury they have done to me personally, the truth of which I can and certainly will maintain. Indeed, by God's help, anyone can clearly see and understand this for himself.

Copenhagen,
The evening of Jan: 5, 1568.

Matters concerning the Earl of Bothwell

The following are the names of the leaders and principal authors of all this trouble and sedition:
> The Earls of Moray, Athol, Glencairn, Morton, and Mar: Lord Lindsay, the Secretary Lethington, the Clerk of the Register and the Clerk of Justice.

Those who joined up with them in these latter troubles:
> Lords Home, Sanquhair, Sempill, Ruthven, Tullibardine; The Provost of Edinburgh, Sir James Balfour.

First sedition
All these people, bored with the obedience and fidelity they owed to higher authority, busied themselves in going about the country, holding secret meetings to build up support for their ideas. In order to gain credence with the ordinary folk that their cause was right and just, they dragged in the pretext of preserving the old Religion. And in this way the conspiracy which they had formed against the Queen [the Queen Regent] – I will not go into the many other things of which they are guilty – began by laying siege to the town of Leith. In this manner they continued to operate as much against the Queen and the Lords of her Council as against all the other loyal subjects in that town. They also persecuted many people who were bewildered by the turn of events and did not wish to throw in their lot with them. These they did a lot of damage to, and pillaged their houses and strongholds. Throughout the whole kingdom they did a great deal of harm to all manner of worthy people, quite regardless of the

fact that the Queen, with her nobles and other subjects, had in the very first instance declared her intention of reforming the religion without restraint on anyone.

Second sedition

Nevertheless, they were not content with all this and carried on with their mischievous plans. To pave the way for fresh troubles, they opened the door to our ancient enemy, the English, making a secret alliance with them against the Queen and the loyal subjects of her kingdom. They laid siege once more to Leith, which they had had to give up at the previous attempt, in an effort to get rid of the French who were defending it for us against these old-time enemies of ours, the English.

Some little time before, the King of France had married the young Queen of Scotland. This had been the occasion for the nobility and other subjects of the kingdom to send the King certain promises, and even writing letters, through their Ambassadors, to his Majesty in France, pledging their faithful obedience as became good subjects. But I cannot think what possessed them to do this.

Meanwhile, because of the help received from England, the town of Leith had been surrendered by a treaty arranged by their Ambassadors, between the Queen Regent of Scotland and the Queen of England. Under this treaty it was laid down that all the old grudges and ill will on both sides should be declared things of the past.

The origin of their hatred and enmity of me

Nethertheless they were so eaten up with their enmity that they never slackened their pursuit of those who had refused to go in with them, or who had got in the way of their sieging of Leith, and above all of myself who, although quite unworthy of the honour, had been appointed Lieutenant-General to the Queen, with special responsibility for affairs of war. During this time I took several Scottish and English prisoners in accordance with the law of arms, and at all times conducted myself as my duty required me. In addition I managed to seize a sum of money on the Borders which had been sent from England for the pay and maintenance of their troops.

167

The Queen of Scots returns from France to Scotland

Shortly after the town of Leith had surrendered and the French had returned to France, the Queen Regent died. On the advice of her friends and at the request of her faithful subjects, the young Queen of Scots at once began to think of coming back to her kingdom of Scotland. She eventually decided to do this, both to reaffirm the conditions of the treaty I have just mentioned, and also to recognise the loyal adherence of those of her subjects who had worked for her during her absence. She was pleased to reward me personally, far more generously and graciously than I deserved: this incensed my enemies so greatly that they employed every falsity and malicious invention to put me out of favour with the Queen. In this they succeeded and I lost much of the Queen's good will towards me. Likewise they got the Earls of Arran and Huntly dismissed from Court, on the pretext that Lord Arran was next in line to Her Majesty and could conceivably succeed to the throne, and Lord Huntly and myself as being most likely to frustrate their plans.

Cunning and underhand work to obtain succession to the throne

The ringleader in all this was the Earl of Moray, an illegitimate brother of the Queen, and former canon and prior of St Andrews. He thought our downfall would be of great advantage to him: if only we could be destroyed, he would be able to carry out the main part of his great plan, which was to become the second person in the kingdom. After that, he intended to get the Queen, together with the nobles and commoners, and in effect, everyone in Scotland, to agree unanimously to his being declared heir to the throne, and after him any children he might have, and after them, all his close relations. This would be if the Queen should die without issue.

And to give some substance to this insolent proposal, he quite falsely put it about that the Earl of Arran (with whom I had just amicably settled some slight difference we had had between us), and I had made plans to murder him and also some other Lords of the Council. Another of his slanders was that I had an idea to take the Queen by surprise and carry her off to whichever of my places seemed most secure.

168

Our imprisonment

As a result of these false accusations, we were ordered into close arrest in the prison of Edinburgh Castle, despite our insistence on the case being brought before the courts and our defence being properly heard, but none of these requests was granted.

The Earl of Huntly taken and killed

The Earl of Huntly, who had been charged with the same offences, was seized as he travelled unsuspectingly about the country, and secretly murdered on the orders of the Earl of Moray. Lord Huntly's son was also taken, tried and condemned, and all the Huntly houses and possessions forfeited to the Crown.

When I heard of this wretched murder and the unfair persecution which followed it, I began to wonder how I could find out what the Queen's real thoughts and intentions were towards me. I discovered that she knew well enough that I had been accused only through motives of personal hatred and envy, but that, for the time being, she was quite unable to give me any help or assistance, since she virtually wielded no authority at all, But she sent a message to say that I was to do the best I could for myself.

My escape from prison and the reason for it

Because of this reply, I made every effort to get out of prison. Once free, I decided to take ship to France, but a tempest drove me to land in England. Here the Queen of England shewed me great friendship as also did several of her closest servants in particular, far more than I could reasonably have expected, bearing in mind the havoc I had created along the frontier during the war.

Some time later I left England to continue my plan for going to France. I was made captain of the Scottish Guard. I had received some letters from the Queen of Scots for the French King and Members of his Council, which made the request that I should enjoy such status and privileges as are granted there to the nobility of my country, according to the terms of an ancient treaty between the two kingdoms of France and Scotland.

I was recalled to Scotland from France

No sooner had I received these benefits than the Queen of Scots commanded me by letter to return to Scotland for the following reasons.

The Queen of Scots marries a young Prince called Henry Stuart

After she become aware of their cunning and mischievous plans, and wishing to put some order into her realms for the general peace and prosperity of her subjects, the Queen resolved to take in marriage a young prince of her own blood who had come to Scotland from England expressly for this purpose. She hoped, naturally enough, that no one would raise any objection to this. Nevertheless, these villains did all they could to stop her, chiefly because they wanted above everything else to prevent her having any children, but also because they wanted no one else to challenge their authority in the realm. They realised well enough that any such marriage could only diminish their own influence.

Third sedition, and the plan of my enemies

Gathering all their friends and accomplices together, they then discussed it among themselves and decided to murder the Prince. Also shortly after the marriage of the Queen and her Prince, these conspirators began to work out how they could capture her and make her prisoner. This they eventually did, in the wickedest manner, quite contrary to their most faithful promises, and even contrary to what they had agreed amongst themselves. This can be seen from what followed.

The conspirators chased off

I had by this time returned from France: the Queen gave me command of a force composed of those subjects loyal to her, and of my own particular friends. With them, I did my utmost to drive the Earl of Moray from the kingdom of Scotland into England. This I achieved. In the meantime the three Estates had assembled to decide what goods and property were to be forfeited to the Crown.

Fourth sedition, for the murder of Signor David

In an effort to prevent this sentence being carried out, some of the Earl of Moray's accomplices who had been keeping a close watch on the Queen's Court, stirred up new trouble. This took the form of murdering Signor David, an Italian, in the Queen's chamber at Edinburgh Castle during supper, when none of her guard was present, not even any of her attendants. And if some others, and myself, had not got out through a back window to escape this danger, we would have been no better treated, as the conspirators had already agreed to do among themselves. At the very least, we would have been forced to become accessories to such a villainous act.

The Earl of Morton, Lord Lindsay, Lord Ruthven, and others

Having instigated this murder, and got it carried out, the Earl of Moray came back from England in the hopes of seizing government and holding the Queen prisoner. His accomplices had already very much restricted her to her own dwelling, called Sainte Croix, or Holyrood.

Their false pretext to justify the murder

As a pretext for the murder, they claimed that they had had express instructions from the King, even letters under his own seal to prove it.

Having got safely from the Queen's dwelling, we collected together some of our best friends, the most loyal of Her Majesty's subjects, and set about rescuing her and her husband, the King, both of whom were now detained. This we did partly by ingenuity and partly by force.

Four thousand men: the Earl of Moray chased out of the country for the second time

The next day their Majesties left together for Edinburgh with a good number of troops and so vigorously harried the Earl of Moray and his accomplices that they had to leave the country. Moreover, the Queen was incensed at such an assassination and nursed a great hatred for them, as also did the nobles and other subjects, but the King himself more than any of them.

Declaration by the King of Scotland concerning the letters and authority which the murderers said they had received from His Majesty.

For as soon as he had reached the city he at once had it given out that everything the murderers of Signor David had said about himself was entirely their own invention.

He gave express orders to all State officials and subjects of the Kingdom to organise a thorough search and arrest anyone who had been with the murderers, wherever they might be found, and punish them with death, and anyone discovered to have helped them in secret was to receive corporal punishment. Also he gave out that everyone faithfully carrying out these instructions would be generously rewarded. Meanwhile, to set an example to others, he had four of those found at the site of the murder arrested, and two of them hanged on the spot.

Their hatred for the King because of his declaration

When some of the friends of those now in exile saw what strict punishments the King was handing out, they lost no time in letting them know. These men, out of their new hatred for the King on this account, did all they could to find a way of avenging themselves on him. This was not only because of his public denial of the instructions which they said he had given them, together with the various letters he had signed to this effect, but also because they realised well enough, as did many other people, that as long as the King was alive, they would never be able to stay in Scotland, in any safety, and that their lives, goods and honours would be always in jeopardy.

Their cunning plans

Some time afterwards, in order to make some progress with their wicked schemes, they promised to forget what had happened in the past, and, by the help of some good friends, they were able to win over those with whom they had been in antagonism and hostility. By such smooth words and good behaviour they solicited the aid of anyone who might be able to help them win back the favour of the Queen, and approached me, among others. In this, I did what I could, since they relied on me because of my high standing with the Queen and the ready access I had to her. As a result, they got what they wanted.

It was as much through the faithful service I had rendered the Queen's mother in her wars, as much as my service to the Queen herself, that I was in such favour: I had on several occasions risked my life and incurred considerable expense, which she had most generously made good to me both by presents and by the appointments with which Her Majesty has honoured me.

My deliberations

After I had obtained their pardon and permission to follow the Court, I thought about retiring to a peaceful life after the imprisonment and exile I had suffered, and having no more to do with vengeance and strife.

Their double-dealing

Meanwhile, those to whom such favour had been shewn, and now following the Court, made themselves so obedient and appeared so kindly disposed to everyone, that all the nobles and gentlemen of the kingdom were delighted, imagining all quarrels at Court to be at an end. But despite all this, the conspirators never lost sight of their wicked plans, and plotted night and day for the death of the King.

Some time after, the King fell ill with smallpox and in order not to endanger the health of the Queen and the baby, he stayed at a house called Kirk o' Field, until he could recover. This was by common consent of the Queen and her Council, who were anxious to preserve the health of all concerned.

Fifth sedition: the death of the King

The traitors now saw that this would suit their purpose admirably. They accordingly collected a whole lot of gunpowder, stacked it under his bed, lit the fuse, and blew him up. This was done at the dwelling of Sir James Balfour, whom the Queen had provided with a handsome living, and also appointed to the governorship of Edinburgh Castle. This included the custody of all her treasure, jewels, silver plate, wardrobes, and furniture, it being the strongest place in the kingdom.

Evidence about where I was when the King was betrayed

The same night that the crime was committed, several members of the Queen's Council were lodged with Her Majesty at Sainte Croix, or Holyrood, as was the custom. I was also in the building, in that part normally allotted to the guard, on this occasion fifty strong. And when I was in bed with my first Princess, sister of the Earl of Huntly, her brothers came in to me in the morning and told me of the King's death. I was very distressed at the news, as were many others with me.

The Earl of Huntly then thought we should immediately discuss the best methods of taking the traitors who had committed this deed.

Thorough search by the Earl of Huntly and myself, at the command of Her Majesty and her Council
At the command of the Queen, who was greatly affected by it all, and of her Council, we were instructed to get a small force together to seek out these traitors and make them prisoner. We set about this at once. And being at the building where the King was lying dead, we first of all had his body taken up and a guard of honour set over it. We then found a barrel or cask in which the powder had been. We put this into safe keeping, after making a note of the marks on it.

In the first heat of the search, we took into custody several people on suspicion, until they could give satisfactory proof of where they had been at the time of the murder. At the same time, I never relaxed my most intensive inquiries to get to the bottom of the whole thing, not suspecting for a moment that I should myself come under suspicion. Several members of the Council, however, afraid that the Queen and I might wish to catch up with them, banded together in an effort to obstruct us.

Their intrigues to shake off suspicion
They used all manner of trickery, posting up bills and placards at night on the courthouse, on church doors, in the streets, and at crossroads, casting suspicion on me and my friends.

My urgent request for a public trial
As soon as I realised that these activities were laying upon me the blame and odium of having committed a crime of which I and all with me were innocent (of which I call God to witness), I prayed Her Majesty and the Council to allow me to stand trial. If, on close inquiry, I were to be found guilty, I would expect to pay the penalty, but if declared innocent (which in all truth I am), such

slanderous attacks should cease. This was agreed to, and a day fixed for me to appear.

My first appearance in court, and my statement

The Council assembled at the appointed place, together with many of the nobility and commoners. Among these members of the Council and nobility who were to try me, there were some who were more enemies than friends. These were the Earl of Morton, Lord Ruthven, Lord Lindsay, Lord Sempill, the Secretary, the Clerk of the Court and the Clerk of the Register. The charges against me were then read out. But then my accusers (principal amongst whom was the Earl of Lennox, who although summoned did not attend) realised that they could not make out any case at all against me, my person, my goods or honour.

My sentence

In accordance with the law and custom of the country, by direction of the judges, and with the consent of those of my opponents who were present. I was then declared innocent and completely discharged from everything of which I had been accused. This was, of course, that I had had any part in the planning or carrying out of the murder of my Lord and Master, King Henry, and that all such charges were without foundation. Furthermore, my own sound witnesses which I had brought forward to testify where I had been on the night in question were upheld.

Protestation by my opponents

When my enemies and other opponents heard that I had been completely acquitted and had won the day, they at once came round begging me not to proceed against them for all the false charges they had brought against me. But their words did not reflect in any way the thoughts in their hearts, as I have since had reason to know, and still suffer from today.

My proclamations on the justness of my cause

For the second time, according to the custom of the country and the rules of war, I had public proclamations made in Edinburgh, and letters sealed with my own seal posted up on the church doors, the Court House, and in other public places, reading as follows: 'For the defence of my honour and reputation, if there is anyone of the nobility or commons, rich or poor, who wishes to accuse me of open or secret treason, let him come forward and I will give him combat in this rightful cause.' But not a man took up my challenge.

My sentence ratified by Parliament
For the third time, I pled my cause before the general assembly of the three Estates, composed of the nobility of the country, all the Bishops, Abbots and Priors, and all the foremost citizens of the Kingdom. There the whole trial and sentence was thoroughly gone over and every point discussed, to decide whether it had been a fair trial or not, and whether there had been any suggestion of fraud throughout the case.

It was then declared by the Assembly that the trial had been properly and justly conducted in accordance with the laws of the land, and that I was therefore to remain acquitted and discharged from all the accusations.

The findings published
Moreover it was publicly decreed that no one, on pain of death, was to repeat those lies or invent new ones about me or mine on this account.

After I had gained my cause, as I have described, twenty-eight members of the Parliament came to me entirely of their own account, and did me the honour of offering me their support and friendship. There were twelve Earls, eight Bishops and eight Lords.

The handsome offers and promises of support made to me by the Members of the Parliament
First of all, they said they recognised that I had done my duty in defending my honour against all the charges brought against me, and that on this account they would employ themselves, their goods, their friends and relations to protect me against anyone who might wish to reopen the accusations against me. Furthermore, each one thanked me particularly for having behaved in such a friendly way towards him. They went on to say that the

Queen was now a widow, with only the one child, a young Prince, and that they would never agree to her marrying a foreigner. It seemed to them, they said, that I was the one most worthy of her in the kingdom. They had thought it over, and had decided to do all they could to bring about such a marriage and would oppose anyone who wished to put any obstacle in the way.

My wife renounced
At the same time they consulted together on how I could put away my first Princess in accordance with the divine laws of the Church and of the custom of the country. They soon agreed how this could be done.

My marriage with the Queen of Scotland
Likewise they discussed the matter at once with the Queen, to see how our marriage could take place before the solemn assembly of Church and Parliament.

The Lords of the Council wished me to travel to the Borders to establish law and order there
The marriage being accomplished, and everything duly and properly carried out, they placed the government of the kingdom in my hands with the wish that I should bring some order into the country, particularly on the frontier with England, where there was so much murder, pillage and larceny on both sides. I agreed to this, and accordingly left Edinburgh with the Queen, who wished to accompany me as far as a castle some seven leagues from the town of Borthwick, where she decided to await my return.

But when I reached the frontier, I found the enemy in such strength that I could achieve nothing, and returned at once to Borthwick (where the Queen was) in order to collect a greater force.

Sixth sedition
When these seditious people, my enemies, saw that I had taken the field with only a small company, they redoubled their efforts to encompass and kill me.

177

Two thousand men

For this reason, I made off quickly to muster my friends and other faithful subjects of the Queen. I did this to such effect that I rescued the Queen from the castle, put our enemies to flight and pursued them as far as Edinburgh, into which they were received. For the city and castle of Edinburgh had abandoned us and gone over to them.

The Earl of Huntly, the Archbishop of St Andrews, with various other Lords of the Council, all of whom had been in the city itself, took to arming as soon as they saw this change of heart, in order to defend themselves against the troublemakers and to save the city. But they were unable to do anything, being greatly inferior in numbers, so we were disappointed in that respect.

When the Earl and the Archbishop found that they could not put up any useful resistance they surrendered to the castle, of their own free will, in order to save their lives, on the condition that they could leave whenever they wished. But this undertaking was ignored by the other side.

In order to rescue them, the Queen and I issued out of the castle of Dunbar with as many troops, faithful subjects of Her Majesty, as we could gather in such a short time, and marched to within about a German league of Edinburgh.

The two forces in the field

The rebels then came out of the town and encamped about a cannon-shot away from us.

They give out their reasons for taking up arms

Not long afterwards, an envoy came over with a written statement of their reasons for taking to the field. These were, firstly: to set the Queen free from the captivity in which I was holding her, and also to avenge the death of the King of which I had been accused, as I have already described.

To the first point I replied that I was not holding the Queen in any captivity, but that I loved and honoured her in all humility as she deserved, and of which she herself could bear witness.

To the second, I replied that there had never been any question of my participating in, or consenting to, the murder of His Majesty. I added that although I had been completely cleared of any charges on this score, if there was anyone of sufficient honour and lineage who still wished to lay accusations against me, I was perfectly prepared to defend my life and honour there and then in the open between the two armies, as laid out in my challenge already published in Edinburgh and according to the ancient rules of war.

I accept the challenge of Lord Lindsay

As a result of this, I was told that one, Lord Lindsay, was getting ready to meet me on the field. But the Queen and those Lords who were with her were not satisfied with this, on the grounds that this Lord Lindsay was not of comparable parentage to me nor my equal in house or lineage. They reiterated that I was a husband well worthy of the Queen.

Nevertheless, I persuaded the Queen and the rest of them so vigorously that they finally gave their assent to the combat.

The challenger fails to appear

Shortly afterwards I went to the appointed place to await my opponent and stayed there until late in the evening without him turning up nor showing any wish to do so. I have the testimony of a thousand men to prove this, if necessary, and can stake my life on it. When night began to fall, I put my troops on the alert and stood my arquebusiers to for the attack. The other side also got ready.

The Queen saw me with her loyal subjects on the one hand, and the rebels on the other, ready to join battle: and the Laird of Grange, who was one of the best soldiers on their side, then reminded her of the reason for this whole confrontation. This, he said, was to release her from the wretched captivity in which I was holding her.

The Queen's reply about her alleged captivity: she parleys with the rebels

Her Majesty openly rejected this before the company. And since both sides were now at the point of joining battle, she was determined to do all she could to prevent the shedding of blood on either side. She therefore went over towards the rebels with the Laird of Grange, to talk with them and see if matters could be settled peaceably. And thinking that she could go to them in perfect safety without fear of treachery, and that no one would dare lay hands upon her, she begged me not to advance with my troops.

The advice I gave the Queen not to trust their fine promises

At this, I begged her to consider very carefully what she was proposing to do and not to let her own good nature be the means of her destruction. I knew well what treachery they were hatching: if she did not agree to all their demands, I told her, they would take her prisoner and strip her of all authority without any justification. Also, I begged her to withdraw to Dunbar and let us fight for her very just cause. This would be the wish of all of us whose only desire was to honour and serve her, and to show our concern for the wellbeing and peace of our country.

A demand for a guarantee of the Queen's safety

But finding it impossible to make her change her mind or listen to any remonstrance, I begged her at least to extract a safe conduct from them with certain conditions which I proposed. The Laird of Grange, who had again come over from them, then gave his own solemn word, on their behalf, to honour these conditions.

False assurances given to the Queen

It should be clearly understood that the Laird of Grange gave out that he had been sent at the unanimous request of the rebels for the sole purpose of offering to the Queen as their rightful superior their true allegiance, and to give her a guaranteed safe-conduct to come amongst them. Furthermore, that each single one of them, whatever his rank or station, wanted no more than to accord her all honour and obedience (after God) in whatever way she wished to command them.

When all this had been most solemnly and inviolately agreed between the two armies in the presence of all the nobility and others there, she begged me to return with my army to Dunbar where she would very shortly join me, or at least would send me news.

And so I took my leave of her, in accordance with her wishes, relying on the assurances and promises of good faith which had

180

been given her, both in writing and by word of mouth.

All things being considered, anyone could see what their intentions were, are, and still are – to usurp the power and authority of the Queen, their natural princess, quite unjustly, and, under the pretext that she had forfeited her sovereignty, to rule the kingdom themselves and make laws as they wished.

The Queen imprisoned, taken to Edinburgh and Loch Leven
This now all being done, I parted from the Queen and she went over to them. They immediately took her and put her in close custody, first at Edinburgh Castle, where she spent only one night, and the next day in another castle on a little island called Loch Leven. This was to prevent any communication between us and also through fear of us making any rescue attempt.

The Council assembles to consider rescuing the Queen
Seeing how the tortuous and treasonable activities of our enemies had succeeded in this way, we assembled together with the various gentlemen and members of the nobility listed below, first in the west and then in the north, to discuss all possible means of setting her free.

The Duke of Châtelherault.

	Earls	Bishops	
The Earl of	Huntly	The Archbishop of St Andrews	
„	Argyle	„	Glasgow
„	Crawford	The Bishop of Dunkeld	
„	Errol	„	Aberdeen
„	Marischal	„	Moray
„	Eglinton	„	Ross
„	Cassels	„	Dunblane
„	Rothes	„	Galloway
„	Montrose	„	Argyle
„	Caithness	„	Brechin
„	Sutherland	„	the Isles
„	Monteith		

Lords	_The Abbots_
Lord Herries	The Abbot of Arbroath
„ Seton	„ Dunfermline
„ Oliphant	„ Melrose
„ Boyd	„ Kilwinning
„ Borthwick	„ Deer
„ Gray	„ Kinloss
„ Ogilvie	„ Lindores
„ Glamis	„ Crosraguel
„ Yester	
„ Somerville	
„ Lovat	
„ Saltoun	
„ Forbes	
„ Elphinstone	
„ Fleming	
„ Livingston	

We were all of the opinion that it would be advisable to wait for a little and not to pursue the rebels too hastily in their present fury, while they would naturally be expecting us to mount a rescue attempt. Had we put this into effect, her life would certainly have been in great danger.

The Council of the opinion I should go to France by way of Denmark
However, it was the unanimous decision of all those present – and those absent ratified the decision by letters under their seal – that I should make my way to France by way of Denmark, where I could gather together everything that might be needed, and make arrangements for the dispatch of troops and naval forces to Scotland. I was also to lay a complaint before the King of Denmark and give him a full account of all that had happened. We all thought that this would be the best way of inducing the King to give me his good advice, help and general favour. As an additional point, it was agreed that I should offer him my service and anything I had in power to give. They were sure that the Queen herself would approve of this move. but to make certain of this, I managed to get details of this plan to her: in her opinion

all the advice given by the Council was excellent, and she begged me to put it into effect as soon as possible.

I embark in the north of Scotland: arrive at the island of Orkney: go ashore on Shetland

This done, I went on board ship on the north coast of Scotland, following the advice of the Council as already mentioned, and having some business to do in the islands of Orkney and Shetland, I put in there, but stopped only a couple of days. While ashore on Shetland, I found some ships from Bremen and Hamburg. I entered into a monthly charter arrangement with their masters, for as long as I should want them, for I had had to leave in such a hurry that I had no time to choose the vessels I wanted, and had to make do with only a few small ones.

The agreement I made with the master from Bremen, called Gerhard Hamlin, was that I should pay him fifty crowns a month as long as he remained in my service. And if during this time the ship was lost, or if I wished to take her over for myself, then I should pay him 'XVI thall' [the manuscript is uncertain here, but its meaning is probably sixteen hundred dollars], with one hundred crowns for the cannons. This can be seen from the contract we made between us. I made the same bargain with the man from Hamburg. But while I was on shore at the house of the Receiver of Shetland, some of my enemies suddenly appeared and separated my ships, as I shall relate.

My enemies pursue me with four ships

The rebels whom I have named earlier on had collected four ships well provided with arms and men. The leaders were the Laird of Grange, whom I have already mentioned, and Lord Tullibardine. At daybreak they entered a harbour at Shetland called Bressay Sound, where lay four of my own ships. When their sailing masters saw the rebels coming, they cut all their cables and made for another harbour further north called Unst, leaving behind all my captains and troops who were on shore.

Meanwhile their main vessel singled out my slowest-sailing ship and set out after it. My ship was ahead, with the others following. But it so happened that the enemy ship and my slow sailer which it was pursuing both ran on a hidden rock. Theirs, which was their flagship, stuck fast, but mine got off, although with some damage.

When I learnt that my enemies were putting in to land to pursue my men, I immediately took them aboard at the port of Uist, which I have already mentioned. I had not intended to stay there, but merely to challenge the enemy. But their three ships overtook and pressed me so hard, as they had already done, that I could offer up no resistance and had to put to sea. I ordered one of my ships, in which was the rest of my silver plate, accoutrements and furniture which I had brought from Edinburgh Castle, to sail to a harbour called Scallow, make arrangements with the ship from Hamburg and both follow after me. As already agreed, I was to set sail for Denmark. They were to pick up the rest of my company whom I had left on the island.

Our sea battle: my mainmast cut: I reach the coast of Norway
The rebels now harried and pursued me so hard that we had a running engagement for three hours. Finally a cannon shot broke the mainmast of my best ship. At the same time a gale blew up from the south-west and took me off course. I was driven on to the coast of Norway, where I was obliged to revictual and refit. Our hurried departure had prevented them being properly provisioned before we started.

It was the day after I left Shetland that I arrived at a place called Karmesund on the Norwegian coast. I was led in by a ship from Rostock, who had followed us during the night to take us into this harbour, since our pilots had no knowledge of it. They also lent us a boat to take one of our cables ashore.

Meanwhile Christian Aalborg had arrived, captain of one of the Danish King's ships called the *Bear*. He asked us where we were from and where we were bound. The master of my ship replied that we were gentlemen from Scotland wishing to go to Denmark to serve His Majesty. I ordered our vessel to pay the usual honours in accordance with the custom of the sea and in deference to the jurisdiction of foreign princes.

The reason I did not wish to declare myself at first
Captain Aalborg asked to see my passport or letters to support our statements. But because I was in such an outfit, as I still am

today, without any of the clothes or equipment expected of one of my position, and since I was hourly expecting the arrival of the ship which had all my things in it, I did not wish to make myself known at first, nor to go ashore until we had reached Denmark. I therefore sent one of my followers to inform Captain Aalborg that because of my lively pursuit from Scotland I had not had time to obtain the passport and other papers which he wished to see, and that she who could provide me with them was in close custody. He then asked if there was anyone in my company who could speak various languages, and, if there was, whether he could come and spend a little time with him. I was perfectly agreeable to this.

He then invited the captain of my ship and various other people to come aboard his vessel so that he could provision our ships and provide us with various other things we needed, giving us to understand that a ship had just arrived in port carrying some help for us. But once he had them all on board, he talked them into staying the night. He then summoned all the country people from round about to come to the aid of the ships of the King of Denmark, giving out that he had, as he thought, some pirates and freebooters aboard whom he wished to take, in accordance with his instructions from the King his master. All this time he gave no hint of his intentions to my people who were with him in his ship, merely giving them the impression that he wished to sail them to Bergen where they could get all they wanted. There was a much smaller company on his ship than on any of mine.

Captain Aalborg goes back on his written promises
He then asked me to allow some eighty of my men to go on board, not because of any poor opinion or suspicion of us, but solely because of the question of provisions which were not to be bought there. He then promised on his honour that he would let each person return to his ship whenever he wished, and gave us letters to this effect signed and sealed by him. He also offered us a safe conduct to go wherever we wished: but he did not keep a single one of his promises.

When we had carried out everything he wished us to do, he separated my people, of whom there were about a hundred and forty, and broke all the promises he had made to us. We had no idea of the reason for this, since we had never given any offence to His Majesty, nor upset any of his subjects, contravened the rules of the sea, nor taken anything without paying for it. I now declared who I was and where I wished to go, but despite this he kept me in custody with the others, much to my dismay. For if I had any suspicion about what he was up to, I could have made quite a different showing against him and his company, since I outnumbered him two to one.

I arrive at Bergen
Having arrived at Bergen, I begged Erik Rosencrantz to help me charter some boats in which I could be rowed along the length of the coast (since I suffered so badly from seasickness) and get to Denmark as soon as possible. Also, if he would be good enough to give me a passport for the journey. Meanwhile I stayed there a whole month, sometimes at the castle and sometimes on board ship with my men. During the next three weeks I used to take walks about the town or wherever I wished, so that had I felt I was in any way guilty of anything, I could easily have gone off anywhere I chose. But I am most grateful to the good Mr Erik Rosencrantz for the confidence he had in me.

I was deprived of my whole company, and then sent to Denmark with four or five of my men
After having waited a long time for my passport, without which I was unwilling to leave, I was told by some of the city Councillors that Erik Rosencrantz and themselves had decided that I should follow the King's ships down to Denmark, accompanied by only four or five of my men, the rest of my company being at liberty to return to Scotland, or to go wherever they wished.

The ship which was supposed to have followed me arrives, but turns back at once as soon as making the coast of Norway
The ship which I had sent to Shetland to pick up the rest of my men whom I had had to leave behind and which contained all my goods, silver plate, accoutrements and jewellery, came along the Norwegian coast. But as soon as they learnt that I was in custody and the rest of the company sent away, they turned back. So I have not only been arrested and detained in various places for four

and a half months, quite contrary to my expectations, since I thought I had come among friends, even though I had no passport, but I have been falsely accused and reproached by my enemies. I have also been completely deprived of all the things which a person of my position is entitled to expect. All of this, however, I mind much less than the contumelies and indignities I have endured in this prison, as well as the way I have been detained without any justification and prevented from going about the business I have in certain kingdoms with various princes and noblemen for the freeing of my Princess. As it seems to me, I have suffered a great deal of wretchedness, loss and ruin at the hands of those from whom I could have expected quite different help and assistance.

At Copenhagen
Evening of Jan: 5, 1568

A second letter written to the King of Denmark by James, Earl of Bothwell

Since I am apparently not to be allowed to speak direct to His Majesty, nor to any members of his Council, to let them know why I proposed coming into the kingdom, I am obliged to put down in writing what I had hoped to be able to say to His Majesty. I trust therefore that the worthy Mr Peter Oxe, Grand Master of the Kingdom, will be good enough to lay this statement of mine before His Majesty.

Firstly: many differences have arisen in Scotland, between the magistrates themselves as well as among the ordinary people, because some of these magistrates under the cloak of religion have been trying to make a profit for themselves. By false and illegal means they have been trying to seize power in the country for themselves. For this reason the country is divided into two parties.

The Queen and I went carefully over this whole situation and came to the conclusion that matters could not be put to rights with the hardest measures which would cause great suffering and bloodshed. We did all we could to prevent such a calamity by peaceful means, and in order to give effect to this, the Queen asked our adversaries for a safe conduct so that she could go amongst them to discuss what might be best for both parties and work out a plan to bring unity and peace to her subjects, to the general wellbeing of the Realm.

To this end, our adversaries and their accomplices gave their written solemn and inviolate promise of safe-conduct to the Lady Mary, the Queen. But when the Queen went over to them, they broke their word in every respect, detaining her as a prisoner and later taking her to the castle of Loch Leven, where she lies to this day. I have already laid this out fully in the document prepared for my defence, which I trust may be placed before your Majesty, in order that he may know the intentions and wishes of the Queen and her Council.

These were, firstly: that I should seek from His Majesty of Denmark, as the ally and friend of our Queen, help, favour and assistance, as much with troops as with ships, in order to release her from her place of captivity.

Secondly, in order to recompense His Majesty for all the expense of this undertaking, that I should be empowered to offer to the Crown of Denmark the Islands of Orkney and Shetland, to whom they used at one time to belong.

Moreover, in order that His Majesty and the Lords of his Council may be fully assured of these facts (as has already been mentioned in my defence statement and also been touched on briefly in this letter) I entreat His Majesty to be pleased to draw up a suitable document, containing whatever conditions, however strict, concerning the handing over of the Islands of Orkney and Shetland such as would safeguard the King and his Councillors of the Kingdom of Denmark to their complete satisfaction. I promise in all good faith that this document will be sealed by the Queen, by myself and by the Council of the Kingdom of Scotland, each one signing with his own hand.

And now I beg His Majesty to be pleased to give me a reply so that I can make good my promise to the Queen of Scotland and the Council of the Realm, which I made at their own earnest request, and so that they may know what they can hope for in their present straits.

. At Malmö
13 January 1568

Attestation of the authenticity of this document by the Chevalier de Dantzay, French Ambassador to the Courts of Sweden and Denmark. M de Dantzay undertook to get the document to King Frederik II of Denmark, since the Earl of Bothwell had been unable to get permission to send it direct, nor to gain an audience with the King.

'I received this document at the Castle of Malmö on 13th January 1568, from Lord James Bothwell, Earl of Bothwell, Duke of the Isles of Orkney, husband of the Queen of Scotland, etc etc, and presented it at Helsingborg to Mr Peter Oxe in the presence of John Fries, Chancellor, on 16th January, whereupon I received a reply from them at the Castle of Copenhagen on 21st of the same month.'

The translation of these two letters is taken from a copy of a text which was at one time in the royal library at Stockholm.

'The undersigned has carefully compared the copy (of the text) with the original manuscript which was actually found in the library at Drottningholm, the residence of His Majesty the King of Sweden and Norway (King Gustavus III).
At Stockholm, 5 July 1828
Signed: P. A. Walmark,
Librarian to the King and Councillor of the Chancellery

Since the latter part of the last century, the contemporary documents, of which there were probably two, have not come to light. They were written in French by a Danish secretary to Bothwell's dictation. One copy was certainly at Drottningholm, as is attested by the King's librarian, and eventually found its way through various hands, including, in 1644, those of an unexplained Doctor Claude Plumius, to the library at Stockholm. As late as 1878, the neatly-written sixteen-page memorandum was still in the library at Stockholm. But now it does not seem to be there.

It seems likely, however, that the Drottningholm/Plumius Stockholm version of the document was a copy of the original which Ambassador de Dantzay had made at the time. It is the

189

text used by the Bannatyne Club for their private publication of 1829.

The more interesting, and almost certainly the original text, was preserved in the charter room of the Château de Pavilly, still the property of the Comtes d'Esneval. This was annotated and corrected in one or two places in what appears to be Bothwell's own hand. These have been printed in this translation as subheadings, for ease of reading. A note on the text in early French reads: 'The said Earl has himself written the annotations which are in the margin.'

The Baron d'Esneval of the time went as French Ambassador to Scotland in 1585.

It was this text which was used by Prince Labanoff-Rostoffski in his famous collection of Letters and Documents, and has been referred to by various historians including M Teulet and Professor Schiern. The text of the Stockholm and Pavilly documents are all but identical

In 1939, the annotated 'original' was still at Pavilly. During the subsequent war the precious library was turned into chaos. More years of patient work lie ahead before it will be known whether this, the greatest personal link with James, Earl of Bothwell, has survived the violence and vandalism of the twentieth century.

Bibliography

I HAVE TRIED to base my assessment of Bothwell on sources as near the original as possible. There is not a great number of these. Later writers, whether historians, chroniclers, or novelists, have usually followed one or two well-trodden trails, often welcoming and perpetuating a personal bias originally expressed perhaps centuries earlier. Some have been strictly impartial, concerned only with recording facts and not injecting any opinions of their own. Others have ignored, adjusted, or occasionally falsified the facts to make their own opinions more plausible or acceptable. It is useful to read as many as possible, provided something is known of the author's likely approach to the subject. The following list is given to show some of the publications to which I have referred, but it is only a small number of the books, pamphlets, papers and letters dealing wholly, or in greater part, with Bothwell's times. I would like to record my thanks to those who have kindly provided me with translations of long passages from works in Scandinavian languages with which I am not familiar.

Anderson, J. *Collection relating to Mary Queen of Scots.*
Bain, J. *Hamilton papers* (1892).
Balcarres papers. Correspondence of Mary of Lorraine.
Balfour, David. *Odal rights and feudal wrongs.*
Balfour, Sir James. *Annals.*
Boog-Watson. *Closes and Wynds of Old Edinburgh* (Old Edinburgh Club: XII).
Boyd. *Calendar IV 655559.*
Buchanan, George. *The Detection.*
   History of Scotland.
Cambridge University Library. Papers: press mark DD 3 66 Buchanan's Indictment, press mark OO 7 47/5 47/8 47/11 Lennox Narrative
Chalmers, George. *Life of Queen Mary.*
Cowan, S. *Mary Queen of Scots and the Casket Letters.*
Crawford of Cartsburn. *A Scots Officer in the time of Queen Mary* (1929).

Crawford of Drumsay. *Memoirs.*

Daae, L. *Christopher Throndssen Rusting* (Hist. Tidsskrift 1872).

de Beaugué. *Histoire de la guerre d'Ecosse.*

de Bouillé, Renée. *Histoires des Ducs de Guise.*

de Brantôme. *Vies des Dames Illustrés.*

Les affaires du Conte de Boduel (Bannatyne Club).

de la Ferrière. *Lettres de Catherine de Medici.*

de Pimodan. *Diurnal of occurents* (Bannatyne Club).

Drummond, H. *Our Man in Scotland.*

Ellis. *Latter years of James Hepburn.*

Fénélon, La Motte. *Correspondence Diplomatique.*

Fleming, D. Hay. *Mary Queen of Scots.*

Fraser, Lady A. *Mary Queen of Scots.*

Goodall, Walter. *Examination of letters said to have been written by Mary Queen of Scots.* Vols 1 and 2 (Edinburgh 1754).

Gordon, Sir Robert. *The Earldom of Sutherland.*

Hansborg papers. Copenhagen Archives: Hansborg XXXIX 28A.

Hardwicke, Earl of (ed). *Miscellaneous State Papers 1501-1726.*

Harleian MSS. Harleian MSS Brit Mus.

Henderson, T. F. *The Casket letters and Mary Queen of Scots.*

Herries, Lord. *Historical Memoirs of Mary Queen of Scots.*

Hollinshed. *Continuator.*

Hosack, John. *Mary Queen of Scots and her accusers.*

Hopetoun MSS 'The Book of Articles' (1870).

Howell. *State Trials. Ormistone's confession.*

Irwin, Margaret. *The Gay Galliard.*

Jebb, S. *De vita Mariae Scotorum Reginae.*

Keith. *History of Church and State in Scotland.*

Knox, John. *History of the Reformation in Scotland.*

Labanoff-Rostoffski, Prince A. *Pieces et documents relatifs au Conte de Bothwell.*

Lettres de Marie Stuart (1844).

Laing, Andrew. *History of Scotland.*

Laing, Malcolm. *History of Scotland.*

Leslie. *Defence of Queen Mary's honour.*

Paralipomena ad historiam.

Lindsay, C. *Mary and her marriage with Bothwell.*

Linklater, Eric. *Mary Queen of Scots.*

Mahon, R. H. (Gen). *The Indictment of Mary Queen of Scots.*

Mary Queen of Scots and the Lennox MSS.

The Tragedy of Kirk o' Field.

Meline, J F. *Mary Queen of Scots and her latest English historian.*

Melville, ed. Stewart. *Memoirs of Sir James Melville 1535-1617* (1929).

Mignet, F A. *History of Mary Queen of Scots.*

Mitchell, C A. *The spurious marriage contract.*
The evidence of the Casket letters.

Nau, Claude. *Memoirs of Mary Queen of Scots* (ed. Stevenson 1883).

Raumer, von. *Elizabeth and Mary.*

Resen. *Konig Fredericks den Andens Kronike.*

Robertson, W. *History of Scotland.*

Schiern, F. *James Hepburn, Earl of Bothwell* (trans D Barry 1875).

Skae, H T. *Mary Queen of Scots.*

Sloane MSS. Sloane MSS Brit Mus.

Stevenson, J. *Mary Stuart, the first eighteen years.*

Strickland, A. *Lives of the Queens of Scotland.*

Stuart. *A lost chapter in the History of Mary Queen of Scots recovered.*

Teulet, A. *Papiers d'Etat.*
Lettres de Marie Stuart.

Thomas, Malcolm. *The Crime of Mary Stuart.*

Tytler. *History of Scotland.*

Weisener, L. *Marie Stuart et le Conte de Bothwell* (1863).

Whitaker. *Mary Queen of Scots vindicated* (1778).

Willocks, M. P. *Mary Queen of Scots* (1939).

Wilson, Dr Thomas. *The Oration* (1570).

Zweig, Stephen. *The Queen of Scots* (1935).

Calendar of State papers relating to Scotland.

Calendar of Border Papers.

Calendar of Documents relating to Scotland.

Register of the Privy Council, Scotland.

Sadleir State Papers.

Proceedings of Scottish Society of Antiquaries (1892-3), (Gilbert Goulde).

Chips concerning Scotland (1817).

New Monthly Magazine (1825).

Additional MSS Brit Mus 3581 folio 129 136-144 146.

'An impartial account of the Affairs of Scotland, from the death of K James the Fifth to the Tragical Exit of the Earl of Murray,' written by an Eminent Hand. For John Nutt 1795.